EIGHT ROYALTY-FREE MINI-MUSICALS FOR KIDS

For Theaters with Not Much Time and Even Less Budget

ROYALTY-FREE SHOWS FOR FAMILY AUDIENCES, BOOK 1

VALERIE SPEAKS AND DALE JONES

Copyright © 2018 Valerie Speaks and Dale Jones

All rights reserved.

ISBN: 1986243680
ISBN-13: 978-1986243681

DEDICATION

For the Dining Table Players, our first readers, who gamely tackled all the wacky characters we've thrown at them..

CONTENTS

	Introduction	1
1	Alice in Wonderland	3
2	Stories from "The Jungle Book"	35
3	The Adventures of Pinocchio	75
4	The Adventures of Tommie Sawyer	111
5	Aladdin and the Magic Lamp	167
6	The Dancing Princesses and the Gardening Boy	205
7	The Secret Garden	246
8	Robin Hood and the Merry Band	274
	About the Authors	313

INTRODUCTION

Looking for kids' musicals that are fun, quick and economical to produce? Look here first!

The classic kid stories adapted here are:

- Alice in Wonderland
- Stories from the Jungle Book
- The Adventures of Pinocchio
- The Adventures of Tommie Sawyer
- Aladdin and the Magic Lamp
- The Dancing Princesses and the Gardening Boy
- The Secret Garden
- Robin Hood and the Merry Band

There are thousands of kids' scripts of *Alice in Wonderland* and *Aladdin* out there, and nobody is going to make a fortune from children's theater. So why are we offering these? Because we know there are lots of teachers and directors who have the kids, the enthusiasm and a stage but very limited time and budget. And our scripts were just sitting on a computer, waiting for someone to bring them to life again.

We created these for a specific need—a summer camp where kids aged 6 to 12 put on a full musical production in five days. They first saw the script on Monday afternoon and performed off-book on Friday afternoon. We had so much fun doing it, we thought we should share the opportunity with other groups.

To make the adaptations budget- and time-friendly, we:

- **Minimized set and costume demands.** Several stories take place on a bare stage, while others have just a backdrop and set pieces the kids can help make. Costumes are often suggestive accessories that the kids will treasure but won't break the bank.

- **Spread the lines around to make memorizing easier.** Pinocchio, Alice and Tommie Sawyer are onstage throughout their stories, but carrying a whole show is a lot to ask of a young actor. So our scripts break the lines up—we have two Pinocchios (Nice and Naughty), three Alices (Small, Medium and Tall) and up to four Tommies (one Old and the rest Young).

- **Used existing tunes in the public domain.** There are so many great, catchy tunes from folk songs and Tin Pan Alley that it seems a shame not to use them. We've created new lyrics and arrangements that support the stories at a very low cost, yet give the kids songs they love to sing with very little rehearsal.

We've brought the stories into the twenty-first century by building in more strong female roles (Maid Marian is an expert archer) and making a lot of roles gender-neutral (Robin Hood can be male or female, as there's a partnership rather than a romance with Marian). Plus we've avoided some problem areas like Injun Joe in *Tommie Sawyer* and the Princes being executed in the original *Dancing Princesses* fairy tale. Throughout, we've tried to maintain the spirit of the original stories, without becoming laboriously "politically correct."

Think of this book as your perusal script. There are eight scripts here for your evaluation and consideration. There's no sheet music, because that doesn't work in this format, but since we use existing tunes, you can probably imagine how many of the songs will sound. (For example, if you know "Beautiful Dreamer," you can hear "Lost and Forgotten" in *The Secret Garden*.)

If you decide you want to mount a production of one of the scripts, visit our website at speaksandjonesplays.com. There you can purchase and download full-size printable script pdfs (including sheet music for the specific arrangements), and/or mp3s of piano with synthesized voice. Once you've bought the scripts and sound files, they're yours—**no royalties**, **no copying fees**, and **no alteration restrictions**.

With the mp3s (that we used in the actual productions), we've thrown in the raw music notation files. If you have *Finale* or similar software, you can change the key, the tempo or the instrumentation to suit your production.

We hope you enjoy these lighthearted productions as much as the original casts and audiences did!

Valerie Speaks and Dale Jones
speaksandjonesplays.com

ALICE IN WONDERLAND
Based on the book by Lewis Carroll

CHARACTERS

Small Cast	Medium Cast	Tall Cast
Small Alice (F)	Medium Alice (F)	Tall Alice (F)
Tiger-Lily (F)	White Rabbit	Cheshire Cat
Rose (F)	Queen of Hearts (F)	Cook w/pepper
Daisy (F)	King of Hearts (M)	Mad Hatter (M)
Violet (F)	Tweedledum	March Hare
Rocking-horsefly	Tweedledee	Dormouse
Bread-and-butterfly	Cards 1, 2, 3 (or just 2)	
Caterpillar	Bottle	
Other Flowers as desired	Cake	Trees as desired

2 M, 8 F, everyone else M or F. Minimum 11, Maximum 25 for everyone to have at least one line.

To facilitate rehearsals, each Alice has her own group of characters to work with in two scenes. Medium Alice also appears in the Opening, along with the full cast.

SET

Bare stage, perhaps a floral backdrop. Add trees, tables and other set pieces as appropriate.

LENGTH

25 minutes

STRUCTURE

Prologue:	Anywhere (All) (Song: Wonderland)
Scene 1:	Riverbank/Rabbit Hole/Hallway (Medium) (No song)
Scene 2:	Garden (Small) (Song: Frolic with the Flowers)
Scene 3:	Forest (Tall) (No song)
Scene 4:	Tweedles (Medium) (Song: Just Use Your Head)
Scene 5:	Garden (Small) (Song: Mosey Round the Mushroom)
Scene 6:	Mad Tea Party (Tall) (Song: Beautiful Butter/Treacle/Pepper)
Scene 7:	Queen's Garden (Medium) (Song: Off With Your Head)
Scene 8:	Courtroom (All) (No song)
Closing:	Riverbank (All) (Song: Wonderland)

Prologue: All Alices and full cast

The ENTIRE CAST enters and sings.

Music 01: Wonderland
Tune: Dreaming (Heiser & Dailey, 1906)
Vocal Chorus

ALL
Dreaming, dreaming,
Of Wonderland I am (we are) dreaming.
Dreaming of sunshine and grinning cats,
Dreaming of tea parties, rabbits, and hats!
Gardens, flowers
All in the afternoon hours.
Nonsense it seems in such curious dreams,
Wonderland!

During the song, the Alices join hands and skip in a circle. At the end of the song, all exit except Medium Alice.

Scene 1: Riverbank/Rabbit Hole/Hallway (Medium Alice)

MEDIUM ALICE sits down and talks to a stuffed cat.

MEDIUM ALICE
It's such a lovely day to be sitting here by the river. *(to her cat)* Don't you agree, Dinah? Why, I'm getting so sleepy!

The WHITE RABBIT runs on.

WHITE RABBIT
Oh dear! Oh dear! I shall be late!

The White Rabbit takes out a watch and looks at it, then hurries on.

MEDIUM ALICE
I've never seen a rabbit with a pocket, or a watch to take out of it!

WHITE RABBIT
Ah, here's my rabbit-hole under the hedge.

The White Rabbit jumps into an imaginary hole.

MEDIUM ALICE
I must find out more!

Medium Alice jumps up and follows the White Rabbit into the hole. The other Medium cast members form the rabbit hole as Alice falls.

MEDIUM ALICE
Oh! I don't seem to be hurt from the fall. I can just see the White Rabbit, hurrying away.

Other Medium cast members become a line of doors, with the White Rabbit running between them.

WHITE RABBIT
Oh my ears and whiskers, how late it's getting!

MEDIUM ALICE
Wait for me! Oh dear, he's gone! I'd better try each of these doors.

She tries each door, which makes a different noise as it refuses to open, then the door exits.

MEDIUM ALICE
This tiny door is the only one that will open.

Medium Alice bends down to look through a small imaginary door.

MEDIUM ALICE
(continued)
Oh, look, it's a beautiful garden! I wish I could go there, but I'm too tall to get through the door!

Two Medium cast members bring on a BOTTLE and little CAKE and form a table holding them.

BOTTLE
Drink!

CAKE
Eat!

MEDIUM ALICE
That table wasn't here before! Why, this bottle has a label that says—

Medium Alice takes the bottle.

BOTTLE
Drink!

MEDIUM ALICE
This little cake has frosting that says—

Medium Alice takes the cake.

CAKE
Eat!

> *Bottle and Cake exit.*

MEDIUM ALICE
Hmm. It doesn't say "Poison," so it *should* be safe to drink. I'll just put the little cake in my pocket for later, and see how this drink tastes.

> *Medium Alice puts the cake in her pocket and drinks from the bottle.*

Oh! Oh! Oh! I feel so strange, like I'm getting smaller!

> *Medium Alice twirls offstage and SMALL ALICE twirls on in her place.*

Scene 2: Garden (Small Alice)

SMALL ALICE
What a curious feeling! I am so small, now I can go through that door into the lovely garden!

The FLOWERS enter and gather around Small Alice.

SMALL ALICE
(continued)
The flowers are the same size as me! O Tiger-lily, I WISH you could talk!

TIGER-LILY
We CAN talk—when there's anybody worth talking to.

ROSE
It isn't manners for us to begin, you know.

SMALL ALICE
I've been in many gardens before, but none of the flowers could talk.

DAISY
Put your hand down, and feel the ground. Then you'll know why.

Small Alice touches the ground.

SMALL ALICE
It's very hard, but I don't see what that has to do with it.

TIGER-LILY
In most gardens, they make the beds too soft—so that the flowers are always asleep.

SMALL ALICE
I never thought of that before!

ROSE
It's MY opinion that you never think AT ALL!

VIOLET
I never saw anybody that looked sillier. Where are your petals?

The ROCKING-HORSEFLY and BREAD-AND-BUTTERFLY enter.

SMALL ALICE
Oh dear, what are those?

DAISY
Why, they are just a Rocking-horsefly and a Bread-and-butterfly. Haven't you seen any insects before?

SMALL ALICE
Well, at home we have horseflies and butterflies, but these are new to me.

ROCKING-HORSEFLY
(examining Small Alice)
What kind of flower is this?

BREAD-AND-BUTTERFLY
And what is it doing here?

VIOLET
Maybe she'd like to frolic with us.

Music 02: Frolic with the Flowers
Tune: Ash Grove (Welsh Traditional)
Vocal Chorus, including Humming Interlude

FLOWERS
The flowers love to frolic!
Come frolic with all the flowers,
Come frolic with all the flowers,
And join in our play!
We dance around the garden,
Our lovely summer garden
Come dance all around the garden
And join us today!

The Insects hum the middle section of the song on kazoos.

INSECTS
[humming and buzzing]

FLOWERS, SMALL ALICE, INSECTS (HUMMING)
The flowers love to frolic!
Come frolic with all the flowers,
Come frolic with all the flowers,
And join in our play!

At the end of the song, the flowers & insects dance off.

SMALL ALICE
That is the most curious experience I've ever had. But it's made me hungry. Maybe I should eat that cake in my pocket. My, look how big it is—it didn't change size when I did!

Small Alice removes a large cake from her pocket (the same pocket Medium Alice used) and takes a bite.

SMALL ALICE
(continued)
Oh! Oh! Oh! I feel so strange, like I'm getting taller!

Small Alice twirls offstage and TALL ALICE twirls on in her place.

Scene 3: Forest (Tall Alice)

Tall cast members enter with tree branches and brush them against Tall Alice.

TALL ALICE
Curiouser and curiouser! I'm so tall, I keep walking right into the tree branches. Oh, there's a cat on a branch!

CHESHIRE CAT enters.

TALL ALICE
(continued)
Please, would you tell me why you grin like that?

CHESHIRE CAT
I'm a Cheshire cat, and that's why.

TALL ALICE
Oh! Well, would you tell me, please, which way I ought to go from here?

CHESHIRE CAT
That depends a good deal on where you want to get to

TALL ALICE
I don't much care where—

CHESHIRE CAT
Then it doesn't matter which way you go.

TALL ALICE
—so long as I get *somewhere*.

CHESHIRE CAT
Oh, you're sure to do that if you only walk long enough.

TALL ALICE
What sort of people live about here?

CHESHIRE CAT
(pointing)
In that direction live some twins called Tweedledum and Tweedledee: and in that direction live the Mad Hatter and the March Hare.

TALL ALICE
But I don't want to go among mad people.

CHESHIRE CAT
Then you'd better visit Tweedledum and Tweedledee, who are only a *little* mad. You're a bit tall for them, though.

TALL ALICE
I could change sizes if I just had something to eat or drink.

CHESHIRE CAT
How about some pepper? Look!

The COOK enters with a pepper grinder.

COOK
Not enough pepper! Not enough pepper!

The Cook peppers the Cheshire Cat, who sneezes and exits.

TALL ALICE
Why do you go about peppering people?

COOK
Not enough pepper! Not enough pepper!

The Cook peppers Tall Alice, then exits, shouting her line.

COOK
Not enough pepper! Not enough pepper!

TALL ALICE
(sneezing)
Oh, now I've got some in my mouth!
(sneezing)
Oh! Oh! Oh! I feel so strange, like I'm getting smaller.

Tall Alice twirls offstage and Medium Alice twirls on in her place.

Scene 4: Tweedles (Medium Alice)

MEDIUM ALICE
How puzzling all these changes are! I'll guess I'll visit the twins, since they're only a *little* mad.

> *TWEEDLEDUM and*
> *TWEEDLEDEE enter and*
> *stand staring at Medium Alice.*
> *She stares right back.*

TWEEDLEDUM
If you think we're waxworks, you ought to pay. Waxworks weren't made to be looked at for nothing. Nohow!

TWEEDLEDEE
Contrariwise, if you think we're alive, you ought to speak.

MEDIUM ALICE
I'm sure I'm very sorry. Are you Tweedledum and Tweedledee?

TWEEDLEDUM
I know what you're thinking, but it isn't so, nohow.

TWEEDLEDEE
Contrariwise, if it was so, it might be; and if it were so, it would be; but as it isn't, it ain't. That's logic.

MEDIUM ALICE
I don't quite understand—

TWEEDLEDUM & TWEEDLEDEE
Just use your head!

Music 03: Just Use Your Head
Tune: Washington Post March [trio section] (Sousa, 1899)
Vocal Chorus, Instrumental Interlude, Vocal Chorus

TWEEDLEDUM & TWEEDLEDEE
Just use your head,
Just use your head,
To think things through!
Be logical, be logical

TWEEDLEDUM
Like me!

TWEEDLEDEE
No, me!

TWEEDLEDUM
No way, nohow,

TWEEDLEDEE
Contrariwise,

TWEEDLEDUM & TWEEDLEDEE
When you just use your head,
You'll be as happy as can be!

MEDIUM ALICE
I'll use my head,
I'll use my head,
To think things through!
I'm logical, I'm logical, you see.

TWEEDLEDUM & TWEEDLEDEE
Like me!

TWEEDLEDUM
No way, nohow,

TWEEDLEDEE
Contrariwise,

TWEEDLEDUM & TWEEDLEDEE, MEDIUM ALICE
When you just use your head,
You'll be as happy as can be!

At the end of the song,
Tweedledum & Tweedledee
dance offstage.

MEDIUM ALICE
Wait! Would you tell me which road leads out of this wood? Oh dear, what shall I do now?

The White Rabbit runs
through.

WHITE RABBIT
Oh! the Queen, the Queen! She'll be savage if I've kept her waiting!

MEDIUM ALICE
Please, rabbit, could you take me with you to the Queen?

The White Rabbit is startled & drops the fan and gloves he is carrying, then runs off.

WHITE RABBIT
Oh! I must run, I am so late!

MEDIUM ALICE
Oh dear, everyone comes and goes so quickly here! What has the rabbit dropped?

Medium Alice picks up the fan and gloves.

MEDIUM ALICE
(continued)
Oh! Oh! Oh! I feel so strange, like I'm getting smaller again!

Medium Alice twirls offstage and Small Alice twirls on in her place.

Scene 5: Garden (Small Alice)

SMALL ALICE
Oh, I'm back in the garden somehow.

The Rocking-horsefly and Bread-and-butterfly enter.

ROCKING-HORSEFLY
You're back!

BREAD-AND-BUTTERFLY
We should take you to the caterpillar!

The CATERPILLAR enters on his mushroom (pushed by the Flowers), blowing bubbles.

CATERPILLAR
Who are *you*?

SMALL ALICE
I hardly know—I'm never sure what I'm going to be, from one minute to another!

CATERPILLAR
What do you mean by that? Explain yourself!

SMALL ALICE
It's just that being so many different sizes in a day is very confusing.

CATERPILLAR
It isn't.

SMALL ALICE
Maybe not to you, but it is to me.

CATERPILLAR
You! Who are *you*?

SMALL ALICE
I think you ought to tell me who you are, first.

CATERPILLAR
Why?

SMALL ALICE
Oh!

> *Small Alice starts to walk away in frustration.*

CATERPILLAR
Come back! I've something important to say.

> *Small Alice comes back.*

SMALL ALICE
Yes?

CATERPILLAR
Keep your temper.

SMALL ALICE
Is that all?

CATERPILLAR
No. One side will make you grow taller, and the other side will make you grow shorter.

SMALL ALICE
One side of what? The other side of what?

CATERPILLAR
You'll find out, if you just mosey round the mushroom.

Music 04: Mosey Around the Mushroom
Tune: Ash Grove (Welsh Traditional)
Vocal Chorus, including Humming Interlude

CATERPILLAR
See, one side makes you taller,
So mosey around the mushroom
Just mosey around the mushroom
When you want a change.

CATERPILLAR, FLOWERS
Or if you would be smaller,
Just mosey a little farther,
Just mosey a little farther,
To find the right range.

> *The Insects play kazoos as before, while the Caterpillar blows bubbles*

INSECTS
[humming and buzzing]

CATERPILLAR, SMALL ALICE, FLOWERS, INSECTS (HUMMING)
See, one side makes you taller,
So mosey around the mushroom
Just mosey around the mushroom
When you want a change.

During the song, Small Alice gets two pieces of the mushroom. At the end, the Flowers, Insects and Caterpillar dance off.

SMALL ALICE
And now which is which?

Small Alice eats a piece of mushroom.

SMALL ALICE
(continued)
Oh! Oh! Oh! I feel so strange, like I'm getting taller again!

Small Alice twirls offstage and Tall Alice twirls on in her place.

Scene 6: Mad Tea Party (Tall Alice)

TALL ALICE
I ended up at the Mad Hatter's house after all! It looks like they're just starting their tea.

> *MAD HATTER, MARCH HARE and DORMOUSE enter with pre-set tea table and five chairs.*

TALL ALICE
(continued)
I think I'll join them.

MARCH HARE
No room! No room!

DORMOUSE
(sleepily)
No room!

TALL ALICE
There's *plenty* of room. I'll sit here.

MAD HATTER
Why is a raven like a writing-desk?

TALL ALICE
Oh, I love riddles! I believe I can guess that.

MAD HATTER
Do you mean you think you can find out the answer to it?

TALL ALICE
Exactly so.

MAD HATTER
Then you should say what you mean.

TALL ALICE
I do. At least I mean what I say—that's the same thing, you know.

MAD HATTER
Not the same thing a bit! You might just as well say that "I see what I eat" is the same thing as "I eat what I see."

MARCH HARE
Or "I like what I get" is the same thing as "I get what I like."

DORMOUSE
(sleepily)
Or "I breathe when I sleep" is the same thing as "I sleep when I breathe."

MARCH HARE
It *is* the same thing with you.

MAD HATTER
Change places!

> *They all get up and scramble around for a new place.*

MAD HATTER
(looking at his watch)
What day of the month is it?

TALL ALICE
Um, the fourth.

MAD HATTER
Two days wrong! *(to the March Hare)* I told you butter wouldn't suit the works.

MARCH HARE
It was the *best* butter.

Music 05: Beautiful, Beautiful Butter
Tune: Beautiful, Beautiful Brown Eyes (American Traditional)
Vocal Chorus

MARCH HARE
Beautiful, Beautiful Butter

MARCH HARE, DORMOUSE
Beautiful, Beautiful Butter

MARCH HARE, DORMOUSE, TALL ALICE
Beautiful, Beautiful Butter

MAD HATTER
On muffins, but not in my watch!

> *The March Hare tries dipping the watch in his teacup,*

MARCH HARE
It *was* the best butter, you know.

MAD HATTER
Have you guessed the riddle yet?

TALL ALICE
No, I give it up. What's the answer?

MAD HATTER
I haven't the slightest idea.

MARCH HARE
Nor I.

MAD HATTER
Change places!

> *They all get up and scramble around for a new place.*

MARCH HARE
Suppose we change the subject. I vote the young lady tells us a story.

TALL ALICE
I'm afraid I don't know one.

MAD HATTER
Then the Dormouse shall!

MARCH HARE
Wake up, Dormouse!

DORMOUSE
Once upon a time there were three little sisters, who lived at the bottom of a well.

TALL ALICE
What did they live on?

DORMOUSE
Treacle! It's like maple syrup, you know.

**Music 06: *Beautiful, Beautiful Treacle*
Vocal Chorus**

DORMOUSE
Beautiful, Beautiful Treacle

DORMOUSE, MARCH HARE
Beautiful, Beautiful Treacle

DORMOUSE, MARCH HARE, MAD HATTER, TALL ALICE
Beautiful, Beautiful Treacle

DORMOUSE
They lived on it, all night and day.

MARCH HARE
Ah yes, treacle is almost as good as butter!

Cheshire Cat enters.

CHESHIRE CAT
Why are you all still here? It's almost time for croquet with the Queen.

MAD HATTER, MARCH HARE
We're not invited.

TALL ALICE
I'm not invited, but I'll go anyway! Only I may be too tall, I think.

CHESHIRE CAT
Here comes the answer to that problem!

The Cook enters, with a pepper grinder.

COOK
Not enough pepper! Not enough pepper!

The Cook peppers the Cat, who sneezes, then the Mad Hatter, March Hare and Dormouse, who sneeze.

HATTER, HARE, CAT, DORMOUSE
Achoo! Achoo! Achoo! Achoo!

COOK
Not enough pepper! Not enough pepper!

Music 07: Beautiful, Beautiful Pepper
Vocal Chorus

COOK
Beautiful, Beautiful Pepper

COOK, MARCH HARE, DORMOUSE
Beautiful, Beautiful Pepper

COOK, HARE, DORMOUSE, CAT, HATTER, TALL ALICE
Beautiful, Beautiful Pepper

COOK
Yes, pepper adds spice to your life!

MARCH HARE
Butter!

DORMOUSE
Treacle!

COOK
Pepper!

MAD HATTER
Change places!

> *They sing a round of Beautiful Butter/Treacle/Pepper as they scramble.*

Music 08: Beautiful, Beautiful Butter/Treacle/Pepper
3-part Round, 1 Vocal Chorus each

> *The Mad Hatter and March Hare start the Round with Butter. Four bars later, the Dormouse and Tall Alice start Treacle. Four bars after, the Cheshire Cat and the Cook sing Pepper*

> *The Mad Hatter and March Hare finish first; they take the table and exit.*

> *Then the Dormouse takes 2 chairs and exits.*
>
> *The Cheshire Cat takes 2 chairs and exits.*
>
> *The Cook lingers to pepper Tall Alice, then takes the last chair and exits.*

TALL ALICE
(sneezing)
Oh, not this again!
(sneezing)
Oh! Oh! Oh! I feel so strange, like I'm getting smaller.

> *Tall Alice twirls offstage and Medium Alice twirls on in her place.*

Scene 7: Queen's Garden (Medium Alice)

Some CARDS enter, with paintbrushes and cans of red paint.

CARD 1
Hurry now, she'll be here any minute!

CARD 2
There isn't much paint left.

CARD 3
There are only a few more white roses.

MEDIUM ALICE
Would you tell me why you are painting those roses?

CARD 1
You see miss, this here ought to have been a red rose-tree, and we put a white one in by mistake.

CARD 2
If the Queen was to find it out, we should all have our heads cut off, you know. So you see—

CARD 3
The Queen! The Queen

The Cards fall on their faces. The White Rabbit enters with a trumpet. The QUEEN and KING OF HEARTS follow. The King is holding a flamingo.

QUEEN
Who is this?

KING
What's your name, child?

QUEEN
Curtsy while you're thinking what to say, it saves time.

MEDIUM ALICE
(curtsying)
My name is Alice, so it please your Majesties.

QUEEN
(pointing at the Cards)
And who are these?

MEDIUM ALICE
How should I know? It's no business of mine.

QUEEN
What?!? Off with her head! Off—

KING
Consider, my dear: she is only a child.

QUEEN
Oh very well. Stand up, you cards! What have you been doing here?

CARD 1
May it please your Majesty…

CARD 2
…we were just trying…

CARD 3
…we know how much you like red…

QUEEN
Silence! Off with their heads!

Music 09: Off With Your Head
Tune: Washington Post March [trio section] (Sousa, 1899)
Vocal Chorus, Instrumental Interlude, Vocal Chorus

QUEEN
Off with your head,
Off with your head,
So says the Queen!
Off with your head,
Off with your head
Right now!

KING
You are the Queen,

WHITE RABBIT
Of course you are,

KING, WHITE RABBIT
But if you take their heads,
There'll be no one left to scrape and bow!

ALL
Off with their (our) heads,
Off their (our) heads,
So says the Queen!
Off their (our) heads,
Off their (our) heads
Right now!

QUEEN
We are the Queen,
How right you are!

ALL EXCEPT QUEEN
But if you take their (our) heads,
There'll be no one left to scrape and bow!

QUEEN
(shouting to end the song)
We are the Queen!

At the end of the song, the King shoos the Cards away. The Cards run off.

QUEEN
Are their heads off?

KING
Their heads are gone, my dear.

WHITE RABBIT
(to Alice)
It's all her fancy, that: they never execute anybody, you know.

MEDIUM ALICE
Well, *that's* a good thing!

QUEEN
(to Alice)
You, girl. Can you play croquet?

MEDIUM ALICE
Yes, Your Majesty.

KING
Then here is a mallet.

> *The King gives Medium Alice his flamingo. She takes it cautiously.*

WHITE RABBIT
And your hedgehog is somewhere nearby—you must find him yourself.

QUEEN
See you on the course! I'll be the one who's winning!

> *The White Rabbit, Queen and King exit.*

MEDIUM ALICE
A flamingo for a mallet and a hedgehog for a ball? Curiouser and curiouser! *(calling)* Here, hedgehog! Come here!

> *Someone hands her a hedgehog from offstage. She takes it cautiously.*

MEDIUM ALICE
(to the hedgehog)
O hedgehog, do please curl up in a ball, so I can hit you with my mallet.

> *The White Rabbit, Queen and King enter.*

QUEEN
She's talking to her hedgehog!

KING
I'm afraid that's cheating, my dear child.

QUEEN
Off with her head!

WHITE RABBIT
Pardon me, your Majesties, but first we should have a trial.

KING
Summon the witnesses!

QUEEN
And then off with her head!

> *The White Rabbit blows on the
> trumpet to call the witnesses.*

Scene 8: Courtroom (All Alices and full cast)

The full cast assembles. The three Alices stand back to back to back, with arms linked. As each witness is called, the Alices turn so the appropriate Alice faces front.

MEDIUM ALICE
I don't cheat! I'm a very honest person!

KING
We'll see about that! Call the first witness!

WHITE RABBIT
Call the Mad Hatter! Is Alice an honest person?

The Mad Hatter comes forward and Tall Alice faces front.

MAD HATTER
She said she could solve a riddle, but then she couldn't.

TALL ALICE
I thought I could do it!

MAD HATTER
You lied to me!

QUEEN
Off with her head!

KING
Not yet, my dear, let's hear from another witness.

WHITE RABBIT
Call the Tiger-Lily! Is Alice an honest person?

The Tiger-Lily comes forward and Small Alice faces front.

TIGER-LILY
She told the Caterpillar she doesn't even know who she is!

SMALL ALICE
I was confused!

TIGER-LILY
That doesn't make any sense!

QUEEN
Off with her head!

KING
In a moment, dear. Next!

WHITE RABBIT
Call Tweedledum and Tweedledee! Is Alice an honest person?

> *The Tweedles come forward and
> Medium Alice faces front.*

TWEEDLEDUM
Nohow!

TWEEDLEDEE
Contrariwise, when she is, she is, but when she isn't, she ain't.

TWEEDLEDUM
That's logic.

MEDIUM ALICE
That's nonsense!

WHITE RABBIT
That's confusing.

KING
And why does Alice keep changing sizes? That's confusing too!

CATERPILLAR
No, it isn't!

COOK
She needs more pepper!

VIOLET
She needs more petals!

DORMOUSE
She needs more treacle!

CHESHIRE CAT
She needs to grin!

MARCH HARE
She needs some butter!

QUEEN
Off with her head! Off with her head!

ALL 3 ALICES
No, no, no, you can't cut off my head!

> *The entire cast swirls around the Alices, repeating lines from earlier scenes, then twirling off. Eventually only Medium Alice is left with her stuffed cat.*

Closing: Riverbank (All Alices and full cast)

MEDIUM ALICE
Here I am on the riverbank again! I must have been asleep. Oh, Dinah! I've had such a curious dream! I wish it had been real! The Cheshire Cat, and the Caterpillar, and the White Rabbit—I want to see them all again!

Small Alice enters and takes her hand.

SMALL ALICE
Maybe someday you will—

Tall Alice enters and joins them.

TALL ALICE
Maybe someday <u>we</u> will—

ALL 3 ALICES
—go back to Wonderland!

The entire cast enters and sings.

Music 10: Wonderland
Vocal Chorus

ALL
Dreaming, dreaming,
Of Wonderland I am (we are) dreaming.
Dreaming of sunshine and grinning cats,
Dreaming of tea parties, rabbits, and hats!
Gardens, flowers
All in the afternoon hours.
Nonsense it seems in such curious dreams,
Wonderland!

THE END

STORIES FROM "THE JUNGLE BOOK"
Based on stories by Rudyard Kipling

CHARACTERS

Opening	Story 1	Story 2	Story 3	Closing
	Storyteller 1A	Storyteller 2A	Storyteller 3A	
	Storyteller 1B	Storyteller 2B	Storyteller 3B	
Curious One*	Curious One*	Curious One*	Elephant-child*	Curious One*
Ensemble A	Mowgli	Rikki-Tikki-Tavi (Mongoose)	Mom Elephant	Ensemble G
Ensemble B	Shere Khan (Tiger)	Teddy	Dad Elephant	Ensemble H
Ensemble C	Mother Wolf	Teddy's Mother	Peacock	Ensemble I
Ensemble D	Father Wolf	Teddy's Father	Leopard	Ensemble J
Ensemble E	Bagheera (Panther)	Father Cobra	Parrot	
Ensemble F	Baloo (Bear)	Mother Cobra	Monkey + family	
	Parakeet	Chu-Chu (muskrat)	Crocodile	
* The same actor plays the Curious One and the Elephant-child. There is no other relationship among how the roles are assigned.				
The Ensemble is an active part of the opening, closing and all stories. Solo lines are labeled A, B, C, etc. and may be assigned to any actor except the Curious One.				

All roles can be played male or female, except for Fathers and Mothers.

Doubling is recommended; you need 10 actors to cover each story. With no doubling, you can have a cast of 30 who all have at least one line.

SET

Deep in the Indian jungle. A backdrop of bamboo trees. The set consists of a campfire (to sit around), a few bamboo trees (to hide behind), and a log or two (to sit on).

LENGTH

25 minutes (2 stories)/40 minutes (3 stories)

STRUCTURE

The script is modular, divided into these sections:

Opening:	Round the Campfire (Song: Under the Bamboo Tree)
Story 1:	How Mowgli Learned the Law (Song: We've Got the Law A, B, C)
Story 2:	Rikki-Tikki-Tavi (Song: Pop Goes the Mongoose A, B, C, D, E)
Story 3:	How the Elephant Got Its Trunk (Song: Down by the Limpopo A, B, C)
Closing:	Round the Campfire (Song: Under the Bamboo Tree)

To keep the show under half an hour, do EITHER Story 2 or 3, not both. For very young actors, do just the Opening/Story 1/Closing and call the show "The Jungle Book."

Each story contains its own prologue to transition from the campfire.

Opening: Round the Campfire

Ensemble members enter and sit around the campfire during the instrumental introduction.

Music 01: Under the Bamboo Tree
Tune: Cole & Johnson, 1902
Long instrumental vamp, vocal verse, vocal chorus

ALL
Down in the jungle we all stay,
To hear a tale at end of day.
Around the fire listn'ing hard,
To hear a story that's filled with glory.
So ev'ry evening we will be
Down underneath the bamboo tree,
To hear of tigers, wolves and bears
And to each other say:
You tell me a tale, I tell one to you
We all hear a tale or two
Every time, every rhyme,
Tells us a tale that's true.
The law of the jungle shows us the way
To live safe and wild and free
Monkeys and bears, cobras and wolves
Under the bamboo tree.

ENSEMBLE A
Who wants to tell an animal story?

CURIOUS ONE
Why do we always tell stories about animals?

ENSEMBLE B
Because that's our tradition.

CURIOUS ONE
Why?

ENSEMBLE C
Because we can learn from the animals.

CURIOUS ONE
Why?

ENSEMBLE D
Because they know how to follow the law of the jungle.

ALL
The law of the jungle!

CURIOUS ONE
What is the law of the jungle?

ENSEMBLE E
There are many laws of the jungle.

ENSEMBLE F
Be quiet, O Curious One, and you will hear about them.

CONTINUE WITH
STORY 1

STORIES FROM "THE JUNGLE BOOK"

Story 1: How Mowgli Learned the Law

STORYTELLER 1A
We know a story about How Mowgli Learned the Law.

Storytellers 1A and 1B stand together.

ALL
How Mowgli Learned the Law!

STORYTELLER 1B
When Mowgli was little…

Storyteller 1B points at Mowgli, who stands.

MOWGLI
As little as me?

STORYTELLER 1A
No, littler.

MOWGLI
Like this?

Mowgli crouches down.

STORYTELLER 1B
No, littler.

MOWGLI
Goo goo ga ga?

Mowgli acts like a baby.

STORYTELLERS 1A + 1B
Yes!

STORYTELLER 1A
So, many years ago…

STORYTELLER 1B
When Mowgli was little…

STORYTELLER 1A
A huge tiger named Shere Khan came into his village…

Storyteller 1A points at Shere Khan, who stands.

SHERE KHAN
Rowr! I want some breakfast!

STORYTELLER 1B
Everyone ran away and hid, except for little Mowgli.

MOWGLI
Goo goo ga ga.

SHERE KHAN
Rowr! Here's a tasty breakfast!

STORYTELLER 1A
Shere Khan picked Mowgli up by the scruff of the neck…

MOWGLI
Goo goo ga ga.

STORYTELLER 1B
…and took his breakfast into the jungle, to his favorite eating spot.

MOWGLI
Goo goo ga ga.

SHERE KHAN
Rowr! I'll go get a drink of water, and then it's time for breakfast!

STORYTELLER 1A
While Shere Khan was gone, two wolves came by.

Storyteller 1A points at Mother and Father Wolf, who stand.

STORYTELLER 1B
They were Mother and Father Wolf.

MOWGLI
Goo goo ga ga.

MOTHER WOLF
What's this?

FATHER WOLF
It's a human-cub!

MOWGLI
Goo goo ga ga.

MOTHER WOLF
Well, we can't leave it here.

FATHER WOLF
Let's take it home and raise it with our cubs.

STORYTELLER 1A
Father Wolf picked Mowgli up by the scruff of the neck…

STORYTELLER 1B
…and the wolves took Mowgli home to raise as a wolf.

SHERE KHAN
Rowr! What happened to my breakfast?

STORYTELLER 1A
Shere Khan got in trouble with all the animals…

STORYTELLER 1B
…for breaking the law of the jungle.

ALL
The law of the jungle!

CURIOUS ONE
Which law of the jungle?

STORYTELLER 1A
Never steal a human-cub…

STORYTELLER 1B
Or the humans may come looking for it, along with the terrible…

STORYTELLERS 1A + 1B
Red Flower!

ALL
The terrible Red Flower!

CURIOUS ONE
What's so terrible about a flower?

STORYTELLER 1A
The animals are terrified of fire.

STORYTELLER 1B
So terrified that they only refer to it as the Red Flower.

ALL
The terrible Red Flower!

STORYTELLER 1A
Only humans can make the Red Flower.

STORYTELLER 1B
That's why the animals are afraid of humans.

STORYTELLER 1A
Years went by, and Mowgli grew and grew…

MOWGLI
I'm twice as tall as Mother and Father Wolf!

STORYTELLER 1B
…so the Wolves arranged for Mowgli to learn the law of the jungle from…

STORYTELLER 1A
Bagheera, the panther.

> *Storyteller 1A points at*
> *Bagheera, who stands.*

BAGHEERA
(very precise)
I can teach the cub the finer points of the law, which are extremely important to know.

STORYTELLER 1B
And from Baloo, the bear.

> *Storyteller 1B points at Baloo,*
> *who stands.*

BALOO
(very casual)
I can teach the cub how to, like, chill out and let the law just flow.

MOWGLI
OK, so tell me about the law.

BAGHEERA
The law of the jungle is very old, perhaps as old as the—

BALOO
Yeah, yeah, it's older than old, dude.

MOWGLI
OK, it's old. What else?

BAGHEERA
The law is our guide in every action we take, whether it is by day or by night

BALOO
Yeah, yeah, it's like this, see?

> *Bagheera and Baloo act out Mowgli's lessons while the ensemble sings.*

Music 02: We've Got the Law A
Tune: Ain't We Got Fun (Whiting, Egan and Kahn, 1921)
Vocal chorus

ALL
Ev'ry morning, ev'ry evening,
We've got the law!
Father, mother, sister, brother
All need the law!
When we're in trouble,
Instead of a claw,
Across the jungle,
We follow the law.
Animals who fight unfairly
Must face the law!
Animals will very rarely
Break jungle law!
There's nothing righter
Than sweet revenge when you face the tiger
In the meantime, in-between time,
We've got the law!

MOWGLI
Wait a second! Do you mean I've got to face Shere Khan?

BAGHEERA
Yes, the law requires that you punish Shere Khan for that transgression in your youth.

BALOO
Sorry, dude, but it's up to you to teach that tiger a lesson.

MOWGLI
How am I supposed to fight a tiger when I don't have claws or fangs?

BAGHEERA
You must use your human weapons.

BALOO
Think, dude. What can humans do that we can't? Besides playing the banjo, I mean.

MOWGLI
Um…

BAGHEERA
What is Shere Khan afraid of?

MOWGLI
Um…

BALOO
What are we all afraid of?

MOWGLI
Oh! The Red Flower! Fire!

STORYTELLER 1A
So Mowgli went to the village to find the Red Flower.

STORYTELLER 1B
The villagers kept their fires in little clay pots, so Mowgli could bring the Red Flower back to the jungle.

Mowgli picks up a clay pot with a stick in it.

MOWGLI
I'm scared to face Shere Khan by myself.

BAGHEERA
We'll come with you.

BALOO
But just for, like, moral support.

STORYTELLER 1A
Mowgli, Bagheera and Baloo hunted for Shere Khan.

STORYTELLER 1B
All the animals helped them, because they all hated the tiger.

STORYTELLER 1A
Shere Khan had broken the law of the jungle many, many times.

Mowgli, Bagheera and Baloo "travel" during the song (maybe into the audience) searching for Shere Khan.

Music 03: We've Got the Law B
Vocal chorus

ALL
Ev'ry morning, ev'ry evening,
We've got the law!
Father, mother, sister, brother
All need the law!
When we're in trouble,
Instead of a claw,
Across the jungle,
We follow the law.
Animals who fight unfairly
Must face the law!
Animals will very rarely
Break jungle law!
There's nothing righter
Than sweet revenge when you face the tiger
In the meantime, in-between time,
We've got the law!

STORYTELLER 1B
Finally, they tracked down Shere Khan with the help of a local parakeet.

Storyteller 1B points at the Parakeet, who stands.

PARAKEET
Squawk! Squawk!

BALOO
What is it, birdbrain?

PARAKEET
Here comes Shere Khan! Squawk!

SHERE KHAN
Rowr! What's this? Are you bringing me my dinner?

BAGHEERA
No, Shere Khan. This is the human-cub you stole many years ago.

BALOO
Yeah, Mowgli's come to, like, totally punish you.

SHERE KHAN
Rowr! Am I supposed to be scared? I could swallow this cub in three bites!

STORYTELLER 1A
Shere Khan smiled and showed rows of bright, sharp tiger teeth.

SHERE KHAN
Rowr! Come forward, human-cub, I am ready for a snack!

MOWGLI
Um…

STORYTELLER 1B
Mowgli was a little scared, but clutched the clay pot with the Red Flower.

BAGHEERA
Go ahead! You've got an unbeatable weapon!

BALOO
Show that old tiger what you can do!

MOWGLI
Shere Khan, you must leave this jungle and go far away, forever.

SHERE KHAN
Rowr! Go ahead, make me.

STORYTELLER 1A
Mowgli pulled a burning stick out of the clay pot and held it in front of Shere Khan's eyes.

Mowgli pulls the stick out of the clay pot. It has red cloth tied around it.

STORYTELLER 1B
Shere Khan whimpered and backed away at the sight.

SHERE KHAN
Meow! Not the Red Flower!

MOWGLI
I will take this stick and throw sparks into your thick, stripy fur if you don't go away.

Mowgli flicks the stick. Shere Khan clutches his/her side as if it's burnt.

SHERE KHAN
Meow! Not my beautiful fur!

MOWGLI
I will burn your whiskers off if you don't go away.

Mowgli flicks the stick. Shere Khan clutches his/her nose as if it's burnt.

SHERE KHAN
Meow! Not my beautiful whiskers!

MOWGLI
I will burn your—

SHERE KHAN
OK, OK, I get the idea. I'm going!

STORYTELLER 1A
Shere Khan ran off as fast as a tiger can go.

STORYTELLER 1B
Which is very fast indeed.

BAGHEERA
Hurray for Mowgli, upholder of the law!

BALOO
Yeah, hurray for using that Red Flower in, like, a totally scary way.

MOWGLI
I hope that tiger learned a lesson!

STORYTELLER 1A
And that is the story of—

STORYTELLER 1B
—How Mowgli Learned the Law.

ALL
The law of the jungle!

Music 04: We've Got the Law C
Vocal chorus

ALL
Ev'ry morning, ev'ry evening,
We've got the law!
Father, mother, sister, brother
All need the law!
When we're in trouble,
Instead of a claw,
Across the jungle,
We follow the law.
Animals who fight unfairly
Must face the law!
Animals will very rarely
Break jungle law!
There's nothing righter
Than sweet revenge when you face the tiger
In the meantime, in-between time,
We've got the law!

CONTINUE WITH
STORY 2 OR STORY 3
OR THE CLOSING.

Story 2: Rikki-Tikki-Tavi

STORYTELLER 2A
We know a story about Rikki-Tikki-Tavi.

> *Storytellers 2A and 2B stand together.*

ALL
Rikki-Tikki-Tavi!

STORYTELLER 2B
Rikki-Tikki-Tavi was a brave little mongoose.

CURIOUS ONE
What is a mongoose?

STORYTELLER 2A
A mongoose is like a cat in its fur and its tail.

STORYTELLER 2B
A mongoose is like a weasel in its head and its habits.

STORYTELLER 2A
Its eyes and the end of its nose are pink.

STORYTELLER 2B
This mongoose got its name because he always says: "Rikki-tikki-tavi!"

ALL
Rikki-Tikki-Tavi!

STORYTELLER 2A
That's who you will be.

> *Storyteller 2A points to an ensemble member, who stands. Rikki only has one line "Rikki-Tikki-Tavi," but says it many different ways.*

RIKKI
(happy)
Rikki-Tikki-Tavi!

STORYTELLER 2B
And we need a family—Teddy, Teddy's Mother and Teddy's Father.

Storyteller 2B points to three ensemble members, who stand as a family.

TEDDY'S FATHER
I'm Teddy's Father. I found Rikki when he was just a baby and brought him home.

RIKKI
(like a cat)
Rikki-Tikki-Tavi!

TEDDY'S MOTHER
I'm Teddy's Mother. I'm glad that Rikki protects Teddy.

RIKKI
(proud)
Rikki-Tikki-Tavi!

TEDDY
I'm Teddy. Rikki likes to sleep with me!

RIKKI
(friendly)
Rikki-Tikki-Tavi!

STORYTELLER 2A
They all lived in a house with a big back yard.

Teddy's Mother and Father move back while Teddy and Rikki move forward.

STORYTELLER 2B
Teddy liked to play in the yard.

Teddy sits down and Rikki wanders off.

STORYTELLER 2A
Rikki would go exploring while Teddy played with some toys.

RIKKI
(curious)
Rikki-Tikki-Tavi!

STORYTELLER 2B
But in the yard lived two big cobras.

Storyteller 2B points to two ensemble members, who become the cobras.

FATHER COBRA
Yess, we like it here.

MOTHER COBRA
But thosse people are in our sspace!

FATHER COBRA
Let'ss bite the ssmall one, sso the big oness will leave!

MOTHER COBRA
Yess, then the yard will be all ourss again!

STORYTELLER 2A
Father Cobra slithered up to Teddy and hissed.

FATHER COBRA
(threatening)
SS-ss-ss!

TEDDY
Help me, Rikki!

STORYTELLER 2B
Rikki ran up and chased Father Cobra around the yard.

RIKKI
(growling)
Rikki-Tikki-Tavi!

FATHER COBRA
A mongoosse! Yikess!

Rikki and Father Cobra act out the song as the ensemble sings the story.

Music 05: Pop Goes the Mongoose A (Traditional)
Vocal chorus

ALL
All around the mulberry bush
The mongoose chased the cobra.
The cobra thought the coast was clear,
POP! Goes the mongoose!

*Rikki catches Father Cobra
and chases him away.*

RIKKI
(growling)
Rikki-Tikki-Tavi!

FATHER COBRA
That'ss enough for me! I'm outta here!

RIKKI
(proud)
Rikki-Tikki-Tavi!

ALL
Rikki-Tikki-Tavi!

Music 06: Pop Goes the Mongoose B
Vocal refrain with ending

ALL
Brave little mongoose
Rikki-Tikki-Tavi!
Father Cobra had to go!
POP! Goes the mongoose!
POP! Goes the mongoose!

TEDDY
You saved me, Rikki!

*Teddy's Mother and Teddy's
Father rush over to Teddy.*

TEDDY'S MOTHER
Teddy, you're safe!

TEDDY'S FATHER
Thank you, Rikki!

RIKKI
(proud)
Rikki-Tikki-Tavi!

STORYTELLER 2A
That's not the end of the story.

STORYTELLER 2B
Mother Cobra was still loose in the garden.

MOTHER COBRA
Yess, and I sstill want to bite that little human!

STORYTELLER 2A
Mother Cobra was so angry with Rikki.

MOTHER COBRA
Firsst I need to bite that mongoosse!

STORYTELLER 2B
She hid behind a bush and waited.

MOTHER COBRA
(threatening)
SS-ss-ss!

STORYTELLER 2A
But Rikki was smart!

STORYTELLER 2B
Rikki heard Mother Cobra hissing.

RIKKI
(growling)
Rikki-Tikki-Tavi!

Music 07: Pop Goes the Mongoose C
Vocal chorus

ALL
All around the mulberry bush
The mongoose chased the cobra.

**The cobra thought the coast was clear,
POP! Goes the mongoose!**

> *Rikki catches Mother Cobra
> and grabs her by the neck.*

RIKKI
(growling)
Rikki-Tikki-Tavi!

MOTHER COBRA
You can't hold me forever, and I'll bite you as ssooon ass you let go!

STORYTELLER 2A
But Rikki held on!

STORYTELLER 2B
Rikki always held on!

ALL
(chanting)
Never let go! Never let go! Never let go!

> *Rikki and Mother Cobra
> struggle, but eventually Rikki
> chases her away.*

RIKKI
(growling)
Rikki-Tikki-Tavi!

MOTHER COBRA
That'ss enough for me! I'm outta here!

> *Teddy, Teddy's Mother and
> Teddy's Father rush over to
> Rikki.*

TEDDY
The cobras are gone!

TEDDY'S MOTHER
The yard is safe!

TEDDY'S FATHER
Thank you, Rikki!

RIKKI
(proud)
Rikki-Tikki-Tavi!

ALL
Rikki-Tikki-Tavi!

Music 08: Pop Goes the Mongoose D
Vocal refrain with ending

ALL
Brave little mongoose
Rikki-Tikki-Tavi!
Mother Cobra had to go!
POP! Goes the mongoose!
POP! Goes the mongoose!

STORYTELLER 2A
That's still not the end of the story.

STORYTELLER 2B
Father and Mother Cobra came back one night and hid under the bathroom.

FATHER COBRA
I sstill want to bite thosse people!

MOTHER COBRA
Let'ss get our revenge!

FATHER COBRA
Let'ss attack together!

MOTHER COBRA
You bite the big oness and I'll bite the ssmall one.

FATHER COBRA
The mongoosse can't fight both of uss at oncsse!

MOTHER COBRA
The housse will be ourss again!

FATHER + MOTHER COBRA
(laughing)
SS-ss-ss!

STORYTELLER 2A
The cobras didn't realize that Rikki could hear them plotting through the house pipes.

RIKKI
(growling)
Rikki-Tikki-Tavi!

STORYTELLER 2B
But Rikki didn't know what to do if both snakes came in the house together.

RIKKI
(puzzled)
Rikki-Tikki-Tavi?

STORYTELLER 2A
Luckily, Rikki had some friends.

STORYTELLER 2B
One of them was Chu-Chu, the muskrat.

> *Storyteller 2B points to an ensemble member, who stands.*

STORYTELLER 2A
Chu-Chu knew a big secret.

STORYTELLER 2B
A secret even Rikki didn't know.

CHU-CHU
(a little slow)
Um, Rikki? Do you want to know a secret?

RIKKI
(impatient)
Rikki-Tikki-Tavi?

CHU-CHU
I know where the cobras have hidden their…

RIKKI
(eager)
Rikki-Tikki-Tavi?

CHU-CHU
Their…

RIKKI
(more eager)
Rikki-Tikki-Tavi?

CHU-CHU
EGG!

RIKKI
(they have an egg?!?)
Rikki-Tikki-Tavi?

CHU-CHU
It's in the garden, behind the big jasmine bush!

RIKKI
(pleased and excited)
Rikki-Tikki-Tavi!

STORYTELLER 2A
Rikki now knew how to deal with both snakes at once.

STORYTELLER 2B
He ran to the garden, then hurried back to where the cobras were just sneaking into the house.

MOTHER COBRA
Look! It'ss the mongoosse!

FATHER COBRA
What'ss he going to do to uss?

MOTHER COBRA
When I'm on thiss sside! *(threatening)* SS-ss-ss!

FATHER COBRA
And I'm on the other sside! SS-ss-ss!

STORYTELLER 2A
Rikki didn't say anything.

STORYTELLER 2B
Rikki just shook his head at Chu-Chu.

CHU-CHU
Um, Mother Cobra? Um, Father Cobra? Do you want to know a big secret?

MOTHER + FATHER COBRA
(threatening)
SS-ss-ss!

CHU-CHU
Um, don't you wonder why Rikki isn't saying anything? Maybe he has something in his mouth?

MOTHER COBRA
What iss it?

FATHER COBRA
Talk fasst, musskrat, or we'll bite you firsst!

CHU-CHU
Um, maybe Rikki has your...

MOTHER COBRA
(threatening)
SS-ss-ss!

CHU-CHU
Your...

FATHER COBRA
(threatening)
SS-ss-ss!

CHU-CHU
EGG!

STORYTELLER 2A
Rikki opened his mouth and showed the cobras their egg.

MOTHER COBRA
That'ss my baby!

RIKKI
(growling)
Rikki-Tikki-Tavi!

STORYTELLER 2B
Rikki showed his sharp little teeth, so close to the precious egg.

FATHER COBRA
Give uss back our baby!

RIKKI
(growling)
Rikki-Tikki-Tavi!

STORYTELLER 2A
Rikki made the cobras promise to go far away and never come back, or else he would bite their egg.

STORYTELLER 2B
Rikki knew the law of the jungle.

ALL
The law of the jungle!

STORYTELLER 2A
Animals have to honor any promise they make…

STORYTELLER 2B
…when they make it to save the life of their babies.

ALL
The law of the jungle!

STORYTELLER 2A
So the cobras took their egg…

STORYTELLER 2B
…and left the house forever.

TEDDY
Rikki is our hero!

CHU-CHU
And Chu-Chu too!

TEDDY'S MOTHER + FATHER
Rikki is a part of our family.

RIKKI
(proud and happy)
Rikki-Tikki-Tavi!

STORYTELLERS 2A + 2B
And that's the story of—

ALL
Rikki-Tikki-Tavi!

Music 09: Pop Goes the Mongoose E
Vocal chorus and refrain with ending

ALL
All around the mulberry bush
The family danced together.
Just when the dancing seemed to be done,
POP! Goes the mongoose!
Brave little mongoose
Rikki-Tikki-Tavi!
Both the Cobras had to go!
POP! Goes the mongoose!
POP! Goes the mongoose!

CONTINUE WITH THE
STORY 3 OR THE
CLOSING

Story 3: How the Elephant Got Its Trunk

STORYTELLER 3A
We want to tell a story about the Elephant-Child.

Storytellers 3A and 3B stand together.

CURIOUS ONE
What's so special about a baby elephant?

STORYTELLER 3B
The Elephant-Child was insatiably curious.

CURIOUS ONE
What does "insatiably curious" mean?

STORYTELLER 3A
It means someone who can't stop asking questions.

ALL
Like you!

STORYTELLER 3B
Yes, just like you, O Curious One.

STORYTELLER 3A
In fact, YOU will play the Elephant-Child!

Storyteller 3A points to the Curious One, who stands.

CURIOUS ONE
Who, me?

ALL
Yes, you!

Someone slips elephant ears on the Curious One.

CURIOUS ONE/ELEPHANT-CHILD
Do I get to have a long trunk, like this?

> *The Curious One/Elephant-Child gestures to show a long trunk.*

STORYTELLER 3B
No, this story is about how the Elephant got its trunk.

ALL
How the Elephant Got Its Trunk!

STORYTELLER 3A
In the beginning of days, Elephants had short stumpy noses like everyone else.

STORYTELLER 3B
The Elephant-Child lived in the jungle with Mom, Dad, and many many cousins.

> *Storyteller 3BA points to Mom and Dad Elephant, who stand up.*

MOM ELEPHANT
Our Elephant-Child is driving us crazy.

DAD ELEPHANT
Questions, questions, all day long!

ELEPHANT-CHILD
Mom, why do we have such big floppy ears?

MOM ELEPHANT
We just do, that's why.

ELEPHANT-CHILD
Mom, what does a crocodile eat for dinner?

MOM ELEPHANT
I don't know. Go ask your father.

ELEPHANT-CHILD
Dad, what does a crocodile eat for dinner?

DAD ELEPHANT
Enough with the questions! Go ask your cousin.

ELEPHANT-CHILD
Which one?

DAD ELEPHANT
Whoever! Just go!

STORYTELLER 3A
So the Elephant-Child went looking for Cousin Peacock.

> *Storyteller 3A points to the Peacock, who stands.*

ELEPHANT-CHILD
Cousin Peacock, why do you have such a big fancy tail?

PEACOCK
I just do, that's why.

ELEPHANT-CHILD
Cousin, what does a crocodile eat for dinner?

PEACOCK
I don't know. Now go bother someone else.

ELEPHANT-CHILD
Another cousin?

PEACOCK
Whoever! Just go!

STORYTELLER 3B
So the Elephant-Child went looking for Cousin Leopard.

> *Storyteller 3B points to the Leopard, who stands.*

ELEPHANT-CHILD
Cousin Leopard, why do you have so many spots?

LEOPARD
I just do, that's why.

ELEPHANT-CHILD
Cousin, what does a crocodile eat for dinner?

LEOPARD
I don't know. Now go bother someone else.

ELEPHANT-CHILD
Another cousin?

LEOPARD
Whoever! Just go!

STORYTELLER 3A
But the Elephant-Child couldn't find anyone who would answer any questions.

ELEPHANT-CHILD
I wish I could find out what a crocodile eats for dinner.

STORYTELLER 3B
A parrot flew down from the trees.

> *Storyteller 3B points to the Parrot, who stands.*

PARROT
I heard that! You want to know about the Crocodile, huh?

ELEPHANT-CHILD
Hello! Do you know what a crocodile eats for dinner?

PARROT
How would I know? Do I look like a crocodile?

ELEPHANT-CHILD
I don't know. What does a crocodile look like?

PARROT
There's one way to know what a crocodile eats for dinner.

ELEPHANT-CHILD
How?

PARROT
Go down to the Limpopo River.

STORYTELLER 3A
The great

STORYTELLER 3B
Gray-green

STORYTELLER 3A
Greasy

STORYTELLER 3B
Limpopo River!

ALL
All set about with fever trees!

PARROT
That's where the Crocodile lives, so you can find out the answer to your question.

ELEPHANT-CHILD
OK. Will you go with me?

PARROT
Just to the near side. You'll have to cross the river by yourself.

STORYTELLER 3A
So the Elephant-Child set out.

STORYTELLER 3B
With the Parrot for company.

The Elephant-Child and Parrot travel while everybody sings.

> **Music 10: Down by the Limpopo A**
> **Tune: Row, Row, Row (Jerome and Monaco, 1912)**
> **Vocal chorus**

ALL
Down by the Limpopo
That gray-green river,
By the Limpopo
That greasy river!
We will find the crocodile,
See his toothy smile,
Ask about his dinner,
Then we'll hurry home in style.
And so we'll go, go, go,
And keep on going till we reach the Limpopo!
We'll ask all that we please,
By the fever trees,
Down by the Limpopo!

STORYTELLER 3A
As they were walking, the Elephant-Child heard a racket.

STORYTELLER 3B
There was a big flock of monkeys up in the trees.

> *Storyteller 3B points to the ensemble, who act like monkeys. One stands.*

MONKEY
Hey hey hey there!

ELEPHANT-CHILD
Hello! Do you know what a crocodile eats for dinner?

MONKEY
How how how would I know? Do I look like a crocodile?

ELEPHANT-CHILD
I don't know. What does a crocodile look like?

MONKEY
Where where where are you going?

PARROT
Down to the Limpopo River.

STORYTELLER 3A
The great

STORYTELLER 3B
Gray-green

STORYTELLER 3A
Greasy

STORYTELLER 3B
Limpopo River!

ALL
All set about with fever trees!

ELEPHANT-CHILD
So I can find out what the Crocodile eats for dinner.

PARROT
Want to come along?

MONKEY
We'll all all all come, but just to the near side.

STORYTELLER 3A
So the Elephant-Child set out.

STORYTELLER 3B
With the Parrot and a whole flock of monkeys for company.

*The Elephant-Child, Monkeys
and Parrot travel while
everybody sings.*

Music 11: Down by the Limpopo B
Vocal chorus

ALL
**Down by the Limpopo
That gray-green river,
By the Limpopo
That greasy river!
We will find the crocodile,
See his toothy smile,
Ask about his dinner,
Then we'll hurry home in style.
And so we'll go, go, go,
And keep on going till we reach the Limpopo!
We'll ask all that we please,
By the fever trees,
Down by the Limpopo!**

STORYTELLER 3A
After a long trip,

STORYTELLER 3B
They reached the Limpopo River.

STORYTELLER 3A
The great

STORYTELLER 3B
Gray-green

STORYTELLER 3A
Greasy

STORYTELLER 3B
Limpopo River!

ALL
All set about with fever trees!

ELEPHANT-CHILD
Where is the Crocodile?

PARROT
Across the river.

MONKEY
You you you have to cross the river by yourself.

STORYTELLER 3A
So the Elephant-Child started across the river.

STORYTELLER 3B
Right before the far bank, the Elephant-Child tripped over a floating log.

STORYTELLER 3A
But it wasn't a log!

STORYTELLER 3B
It was the Crocodile!

ALL
The Crocodile!

Storyteller 3B points to the Crocodile, who stands.

CROCODILE
Who is that, splashing and kicking me?

ELEPHANT-CHILD
Excuse me! Do you know what a crocodile eats for dinner?

CROCODILE
Why do you ask? Do I look like a crocodile?

ELEPHANT-CHILD
I don't know. What does a crocodile look like?

CROCODILE
Well, a crocodile lives in the river…

ALL
Like you!

CROCODILE
…and looks a little like a floating log…

ALL
Like you!

CROCODILE
…and has a long toothy smile…

ALL
Like you!

ELEPHANT-CHILD
Oh, it's you!

CROCODILE
Yes, I am the Crocodile.

ELEPHANT-CHILD
Please tell me what I long to know! What do you eat for dinner?

CROCODILE
I'll tell you, but you have to lean down so I can whisper it in your ear.

ELEPHANT-CHILD
Tell me, tell me!

STORYTELLER 3A
The Elephant-Child leaned over, with those big floppy ears…

STORYTELLER 3B
…and that short stumpy nose.

CROCODILE
Closer, I can't whisper that loud.

ELEPHANT-CHILD
Tell me, tell me!

STORYTELLER 3A
The Elephant-Child leaned down further…

STORYTELLER 3B
…and further.

CROCODILE
Still closer, it's such a secret.

ELEPHANT-CHILD
Tell me, tell me!

STORYTELLER 3A
The Elephant-Child leaned down even further…

STORYTELLER 3B
…right next to the Crocodile's grinning face.

STORYTELLER 3A
And the Crocodile bit down, SNAP!

ALL
SNAP!

STORYTELLER 3B
Right on the Elephant-Child's short, stumpy nose!

ALL
SNAP!

ELEPHANT-CHILD
(with stuffy nose)
Ow! Stob dat blease. Ow Ow Ow!

CROCODILE
(through clenched teeth)
To answer your question: for dinner tonight I will have some Elephant-Child!

STORYTELLER 3A
The Elephant-Child leaned back, but the Crocodile was stronger.

STORYTELLER 3B
The Elephant-Child was being pulled into the water.

ELEPHANT-CHILD
Hep! Hep!

STORYTELLER 3A
The Parrot and Monkeys heard the Elephant-Child and rushed over the river.

MONKEY
Hey hey hey we'll help you!

STORYTELLER 3B
The Monkeys helped the Elephant-Child pull, while the Parrot flew off for help.

PARROT
Help! Elephants! Cousins! Help!

STORYTELLER 3A
The Elephant-Child's nose was being pulled very hard.

ELEPHANT-CHILD
Ow Ow Ow!

STORYTELLER 3B
Meanwhile, the Cousins and Mom and Dad came to help with the pulling.

It's a tug-of-war between the Crocodile and the family, with the Elephant-Child's nose in the middle. The Elephant-Child slips on a trunk.

STORYTELLER 3A
The Crocodile pulled and pulled the Elephant-Child toward the water…

STORYTELLER 3B
…while everyone else pulled and pulled the other way.

ELEPHANT-CHILD
Ow Ow Ow!

STORYTELLER 3A
And the Elephant-Child's nose got longer and longer.

STORYTELLER 3B
It wasn't short and stumpy anymore!

ELEPHANT-CHILD
Ow Ow Ow!

Finally the Crocodile lets go. Everyone collapses.

CROCODILE
Oh, forget it. I'll go find something easier for dinner.

LEOPARD
Thank goodness the Crocodile is gone!

PEACOCK
But look at that nose!

MONKEY
I I I like it!

PARROT
I wonder what you can do with it.

ELEPHANT-CHILD
Look, I can reach things that are far away…

ALL
Advantage number one!

ELEPHANT-CHILD
I can squirt water with it…

ALL
Advantage number two!

ELEPHANT-CHILD
And I can make a trumpet noise with it…

> *The Elephant-Child makes a trumpet noise.*

ALL
Advantage number three?!?

MOM ELEPHANT
Hmm, maybe we should go see the Crocodile…

DAD ELEPHANT
…and get new noses for ourselves!

STORYTELLER 3A
And that is why all the elephants you will ever see…

STORYTELLER 3B
…plus all the ones you'll never see…

STORYTELLERS 3A + 3B
Have a long trunk!

> *The Elephant-Child takes off the ears/nose.*

CURIOUS ONE
But why did all the Cousins come help, when the Elephant-Child was such a pest?

STORYTELLER 3A
Because they knew the law of the jungle!

STORYTELLER 3B
An important law of the jungle!

CURIOUS ONE
What's that?

Storyteller 3A puts the ears/nose on the Curious One.

STORYTELLER 3A
No matter how much your relatives annoy you…

STORYTELLER 3B
…you must always come to their rescue.

ALL
The law of the jungle!

Music 12: Down by the Limpopo C
Vocal chorus

ALL
Down by the Limpopo
That gray-green river,
By the Limpopo
That greasy river!
We will find the crocodile,
See his toothy smile,
Ask about his dinner,
Then we'll hurry home in style.
And so we'll go, go, go,
And keep on going till we reach the Limpopo!
We'll ask all that we please,
By the fever trees,
Down by the Limpopo!

CONTINUE WITH THE CLOSING

Closing: Round the Campfire

ENSEMBLE G
So that's the end of our storytelling for tonight.

CURIOUS ONE
Aw, can't we do some more?

ENSEMBLE H
We have to save some stories for tomorrow.

ENSEMBLE I
And the night after that.

ENSEMBLE J
There's so much to know about the law.

ALL
The law of the jungle!

Music 13: Under the Bamboo Tree
Vocal chorus with ending

ALL
You tell me a tale, I tell one to you
We all hear a tale or two
Every time, every rhyme,
Tells us a tale that's true.
The law of the jungle shows us the way
To live safe and wild and free
Monkeys and bears, cobras and wolves
Under the bamboo tree.

Monkeys and bears, cobras and wolves
Under the bamboo tree.

THE END

THE ADVENTURES OF PINOCCHIO
Based on the book by Carlo Collodi
Additional Lyrics by Stacia Martin

CHARACTERS

Blue Fairy	F	Leader of the fairies
Pink Fairy	F	Fairies in training. Pink & Purple are cheery; Silver is a smart aleck.
Purple Fairy	F	
Silver Fairy	F	(Plus other fairies as desired)
Geppetto	M	Poor woodcarver
Nice Pinocchio	M (or F playing M)	Short-nosed puppet who wants to be a real boy
Cricket	M or F	Talking insect who tries to help Pinocchio
Cheesemaker	M or F	Townsfolk
Baker	M or F	The Fox, Cat, Coach Driver, Lampwick, Unruly Kids and Whale double as townsfolk, adding special costume pieces for when they play their named roles.
Olive Grower	M or F	
Tailor	M or F	
Shoemaker	M or F	
Hatmaker	M or F	
Naughty Pinocchio	M (or F playing M)	Long-nosed puppet who tells lies and gets in trouble
Fox	M or F	Sly trickster
Cat	M or F	Echoes everything the Fox says
Coach Driver	M or F	Overly friendly childnapper
Lampwick	M	Mischievous kids (number open)
Unruly Kids	M & F	
Whale	M & F	Multiple actors, depending on how the whale is built

2 M, 4 F, 6-12 M or F

12 with doubling, 18 without. Plus Unruly Kids and Whale singers (number open)

SET

Once upon a time in an Italian village

All set pieces need to be easily pushed or rolled, and have space for Pinocchio to hide behind them.

- Geppetto's cart (with wooden items and space for Nice Pinocchio to sit)
- Magic tree (with spot to place a penny)
- Fun Land Wagon (with space to store donkey ears)
- Whale (not really a set piece, more like a Chinese parade dragon; when the mouth opens, we can see Geppetto's face inside)
- "Mirror" (a rolling frame that allows the Pinocchios to do the reflection routine)

LENGTH

30 minutes

Once Upon a Time in an Italian Village

A group of FAIRIES enter, led by the BLUE FAIRY, who has a full magical wand. The other fairies have no stars on their wands. They sing as they flitter about.

> **Music 01: Song of the Fairies**
> **Tune: Dance of the Hours (from "La Gioconda" by Ponchielli, 1876)**
> **Instrumental chorus, Vocal chorus**

ALL FAIRIES
See us flutter
See us flitter
See our magic
Make us glitter!
We bring gladness
To the sad ones
And bring sorry thoughts
To sadden all the bad ones!

The Fairies in Training gather around the Blue Fairy.

BLUE FAIRY
Sisters, you are almost through with your training.

FAIRIES IN TRAINING
Yay!

BLUE FAIRY
Soon you will earn stars for your wands!

FAIRIES IN TRAINING
Yay!

BLUE FAIRY
You just need to help one more human to be happy!

FAIRIES IN TRAINING
Yay!

PINK FAIRY
I can't wait until we get our stars!

PURPLE FAIRY
We will do so much good magic!

SILVER FAIRY
Yeah, yeah, but who are we supposed to help?

BLUE FAIRY
Look at all the people in this village. You will help one of them.

Music 02: Village Parade (Same arrangement as Music 07)
Tune: Carnival of Venice (Italian folk song)
Vocal chorus, Instrumental dance

The TOWNSFOLK (including the CHEESEMAKER, BAKER, OLIVE GROWER, TAILOR, SHOEMAKER and HATMAKER) dance by.

TOWNSFOLK
We're happy in our village,
Oh so happy all the time!
The sun shines all day in our village,
To be sad would be a crime!

The Townsfolk speak over the instrumental dance music.

CHEESEMAKER
I make the best cheese in the village!

BAKER
I bake the bread to go with the cheese!

OLIVE GROWER
I make the olive oil to go with the bread!

TAILOR
Stop, you're making me hungry!

SHOEMAKER
I'm hungry too!

HATMAKER
I could eat a horse!

ALL TOWNSFOLK
Let's go eat!

Townsfolk exit.

BLUE FAIRY
(pointing)
There's the right human for you to help!

GEPPETTO enters, sadly pushing a cart loaded with wooden items. NICE PINOCCHIO is sitting on the cart, slumped over like a puppet. NAUGHTY PINOCCHIO is hidden behind the cart. The CRICKET follows.

PINK FAIRY
Oh, he looks so sad!

GEPPETTO
Well, another day with no one buying my carvings.

CRICKET
Crick-ette!

PURPLE FAIRY
And no one to talk to but a cricket!

GEPPETTO
(to Nice Pinocchio)
Too bad you can't hear me, little puppet. You are my favorite carving.

CRICKET
Crick-ette!

SILVER FAIRY
Hey, maybe we could make the cricket talk with our magic!

BLUE FAIRY
I think Geppetto would be happier if you made the puppet talk.

PINK FAIRY
Good idea!

PURPLE FAIRY
Do we have enough magic to do that?

BLUE FAIRY
You can do it if you work together.

SILVER FAIRY
Well, I still think we should make the <u>cricket</u> talk.

OTHER FAIRIES
Ssh!

GEPPETTO
I will go get some water for our dinner. There won't be much to eat, I'm afraid.

CRICKET
Crick-ette!

Geppetto exits. The fairies gather around Nice Pinocchio.

BLUE FAIRY
On the count of three.

FAIRIES IN TRAINING
One, two, three!

The Fairies in Training wave their wands together.

SFX: Fairy Magic (Loud)

Nice Pinocchio sits up and rubs his eyes. The Cricket is astonished.

CRICKET
Crick-ette!

NICE PINOCCHIO
Hello! What am I doing up here?

FAIRIES IN TRAINING
Yay!

BLUE FAIRY
Let's go, sisters!

PINK FAIRY
That was fun!

PURPLE FAIRY
I hope it makes Geppetto happy!

The Fairies in Training exit.
The Blue Fairy lingers.

BLUE FAIRY
Little puppet, now you can walk and talk.

NICE PINOCCHIO
Yes, I can!

CRICKET
Crick-ette!

BLUE FAIRY
But you're not a real boy yet.

NICE PINOCCHIO
Why not?

BLUE FAIRY
Prove that you can be a good son to Geppetto, and you will become real.

NICE PINOCCHIO
Good? I guess I can do that.

CRICKET
Crick-ette!

BLUE FAIRY
Good luck, little puppet! We'll be watching you!

The Blue Fairy exits while the
Silver Fairy sneaks back on.

SILVER FAIRY
Here, Cricket, this is for you.

The Silver Fairy waves her
wand and exits.

SFX: Fairy Magic (Soft)

CRICKET
Hello! Hello! Crick-ette!

NICE PINOCCHIO
Hello! Who are you?

CRICKET
I seem to be a talking cricket. Who are you?

NICE PINOCCHIO
(looking down at himself)
I seem to be a talking puppet!

Geppetto enters with a water container.

NICE PINOCCHIO
Hello!

Geppetto jumps in shock.

GEPPETTO
Who is talking?

CRICKET
Hello there! Crick-ette!

Geppetto jumps even higher in shock.

GEPPETTO
A talking cricket! It's a miracle!

NICE PINOCCHIO
Look at me! I talk too!

Geppetto jumps as high as possible and drops the water.

GEPPETTO
A talking puppet! It's what I wished for!

NICE PINOCCHIO
Help me down from here. I want to walk!

CRICKET
You should say "please" to your father. That's what good boys do.

NICE PINOCCHIO
I do want to be good. Please, Father?

GEPPETTO
Anything for you, my boy!

Geppetto helps Nice Pinocchio down.

NICE PINOCCHIO
Am I your boy?

GEPPETTO
You will be my son. I will call you—

CRICKET
Peter Pan?

GEPPETTO
No, wrong story.

NICE PINOCCHIO
Willy Wonka?

GEPPETTO
No, wrong story.

CRICKET
Rumplestiltskin?

GEPPETTO
No, no. I know! Pinocchio!

NICE PINOCCHIO, CRICKET
Pinocchio!

During the song, Nice Pinocchio practices walking and dancing, with the Cricket and Geppetto showing him how.

> **Music 03: Oh My Pinocchio (Same arrangement as Music 06)**
> **Tune: Santa Lucia (Italian folk song)**
> **Vocal chorus**

GEPPETTO
Oh my Pinocchio,
That name does please me so!
You mean the world to me,
We'll be a family.

NICE PINOCCHIO
Call me Pinocchio,
That name does please me so!

CRICKET
More than a puppet now,
Why don't you take a bow?

GEPPETTO, NICE PINOCCHIO, CRICKET
See how you (I) walk around,
See how you (I) run and bound
No strings to tie you down!
Yes, you're (I'm) Pinocchio!

GEPPETTO
Well, my boy, the first thing you need is to go to school.

NICE PINOCCHIO
School? That sounds like work!

CRICKET
Good boys go to school.

NICE PINOCCHIO
They do? Every day?

GEPPETTO
Yes, they do! Here is my last penny to buy a schoolbook.

Geppetto gives Nice Pinocchio a penny.

GEPPETTO
I'll see you when you come home, dear Pinocchio.

> *Geppetto exits, humming and dancing a little.*

NICE PINOCCHIO
(calling after Geppetto)
Yes, Father. I really <u>want</u> to go to school. Oh! Oh! Oh!

CRICKET
What is happening to your nose?

SFX: Nose Growing Music

> *Nice Pinocchio holds his hands over his nose and staggers behind the cart. NAUGHTY PINOCCHIO emerges from the other side with his hands over his nose.*

NAUGHTY PINOCCHIO
Oh! Oh! Oh!

> *When he takes his hands down, we can see how long his nose has become.*

CRICKET
Your nose is getting longer! That's what happens when you tell lies!

NAUGHTY PINOCCHIO
Ha! I don't care! I like being naughty!

Music 04: Naughty Pinocchio/Village Parade Lines, Underscoring from Oh My Pinocchio/ Vocal chorus, Instrumental dance from Village Parade

CRICKET
Naughty Pinocchio,
Naughty Pinocchio!

NAUGHTY PINOCCHIO
(over the music)
I'm going outside to explore, and you can't stop me!

CRICKET
Naughty Pinocchio,
Naughty Pinocchio!

> *Naughty Pinocchio walks away.
> The Townsfolk (now including
> the FOX and CAT) enter.
> Someone rolls the cart offstage,
> with Nice Pinocchio hiding
> behind it.*

NAUGHTY PINOCCHIO
(over the music)
Look at all these people!

CRICKET
Wait! You have to go to school!

NAUGHTY PINOCCHIO
No! I'm going to have an adventure, and I don't need you!

CRICKET
Wait! What about the money Geppetto gave you?

NAUGHTY PINOCCHIO
I'll spend it any way I want! Now go!

> *The Cricket exits sadly. The
> Fox and Cat have overheard the
> talk of money.*

TOWNSFOLK
We're happy in our village,
Oh so happy all the time!
The sun shines all day in our village,
To be sad would be a crime!

> *Over the instrumental music, the
> Townsfolk call to Naughty
> Pinocchio.*

TAILOR
Come dance with me! I'll make you a new suit!

SHOEMAKER
I'll make you the best shoes you ever danced in!

HATMAKER
I'll make you a sharp new hat with a feather!

CHEESEMAKER
You'll be so handsome!

BAKER
You'll look like a new puppet!

OLIVE GROWER
You'll be the finest dancer in the village!

ALL TOWNSFOLK
Let's keep dancing!

At the end of the dance, the Fox and Cat surround Naughty Pinocchio and keep him onstage as the Townsfolk exit.

NAUGHTY PINOCCHIO
This is so much more fun than going to school!

FOX
Yes, isn't it fun to dance and sing?

CAT
Dance and sing?

NAUGHTY PINOCCHIO
Yes!

FOX
Going to school is just for boring people.

CAT
Boring people.

NAUGHTY PINOCCHIO
Yes! Yes!

FOX
We can help you have lots of fun!

CAT
Lots of fun!

NAUGHTY PINOCCHIO
Yes! Yes! Yes!

FOX
It only costs three pennies.

CAT
Three pennies.

NAUGHTY PINOCCHIO
Oh too bad, I only have one penny.

Naughty Pinocchio turns away sadly. The Fox and Cat look at each other and get an idea, then pull Naughty Pinocchio back.

FOX
We can help you turn one penny into three.

CAT
One penny into three.

NAUGHTY PINOCCHIO
You can?

Music 05: One Penny Into Three
Tune: Tarantella (Italian wedding song)
Vocal chorus, underscoring, vocal finish

FOX
First, you find the magic tree,

CAT
Find the magic, magic tree

FOX
Put your money in the ground,
And your penny turns into three!
One!

CAT
Two!

They look at Naughty Pinocchio, who is obviously supposed to yell "Three!" but doesn't. The Fox continues.

FOX
Then you take a little nap,

CAT
Take a little, little nap.

FOX
When you wake up, you will see
How your penny turns into three!
One!

CAT
Two!

NAUGHTY PINOCCHIO
Three!

During the following, the Fox, Cat and Naughty Pinocchio "walk" in place. A tree slides on as if they are approaching it. (Nice Pinocchio is hidden behind the tree.)

NAUGHTY PINOCCHIO
When I wake up, I will have some money,
Lots spend on toys and honey,
Candy, games and flow'rs.
(pointing at the tree)
Is this the tree with the magic pow'rs?

FOX
Yes!

CAT
Yes!

NAUGHTY PINOCCHIO
Three!

During the following, Naughty Pinocchio places his penny at the foot of the tree, then curls up nearby for a nap.

FOX
(quietly)
Then you take a little nap,

CAT
(quietly)
Take a little, little nap.

FOX
**When you wake up, you will see
How your penny turns into three!
One!**

CAT
Two!

NAUGHTY PINOCCHIO
(sleepily)
Three!

FOX, CAT
Hush!

Naughty Pinocchio is sound asleep. As the music continues, the Fox tiptoes over and picks up the penny.

FOX
Take this penny into town,

CAT
Take this penny into town,

FOX
**While we gamble, we will see
How this penny turns into three!
One!**

CAT
Two!

FOX, CAT
Three!

The Fox and Cat laugh and tiptoe offstage.

The Cricket and Geppetto run on.

GEPPETTO
Pinocchio!

CRICKET
Over here, fairies!

The Fairies in Training enter.

PINK FAIRY
There he is!

PURPLE FAIRY
Thank goodness we found him!

SILVER FAIRY
Look at his nose! It's ridiculous!

Naughty Pinocchio wakes up and looks for his money.

NAUGHTY PINOCCHIO
What happened to my penny?

GEPPETTO
Oh, Pinocchio. Did you lose that money?

NAUGHTY PINOCCHIO
I put it here, where the Fox told me to.

CRICKET
Oh, Pinocchio. Everyone knows you can't trust that Fox.

NAUGHTY PINOCCHIO
Oh.

GEPPETTO
I'm just glad we found you, Pinocchio. Come on home.

CRICKET
(to the Fairies)
Can't you fix his nose?

PINK FAIRY
We can try.

PURPLE FAIRY
We're still in training.

SILVER FAIRY
I think it serves him right.

OTHER FAIRIES
Ssh!

FAIRIES IN TRAINING
One, two, three!

> *The Fairies in Training wave their wands together.*

SFX: Fairy Magic (Loud)

> *Naughty Pinocchio sneezes, but his nose doesn't shrink.*

NAUGHTY PINOCCHIO
Achoo! Stop! That tickles!

FAIRIES IN TRAINING
Help! Blue Fairy, we need you!

CRICKET & GEPPETTO
Help! Blue Fairy!

> *The Blue Fairy enters.*

BLUE FAIRY
So, little puppet, you have gotten into trouble already.

CRICKET
He told a lie, and his nose grew like that!

BLUE FAIRY
I see. Well, little puppet, do you want to be good?

NAUGHTY PINOCCHIO
Yes I do! Please help me, Blue Fairy!

BLUE FAIRY
Then we'll give you a second chance. Ready, sisters?

ALL FAIRIES
One, two, three!

The Fairies wave their wands together.

SFX: Fairy Magic & Nose Shrinking Music

Naughty Pinocchio holds his hands over his nose and staggers behind the tree. Nice Pinocchio emerges from the other side with his hands over his nose.

NICE PINOCCHIO
Oh! Oh! Oh!

When he takes his hands down, we can see how short his nose has become.

GEPPETTO
Pinocchio!

CRICKET
Pinocchio!

NICE PINOCCHIO
Look, Father, my nose is nice and small again!

Geppetto hugs Nice Pinocchio.

PINK FAIRY
How sweet!

PURPLE FAIRY
I'm so glad we could help!

The Fairies in Training exit, except the Silver Fairy who lingers.

SILVER FAIRY
(to Nice Pinocchio)
Don't expect us to come back if you get into trouble again! We have better things to do!

Silver Fairy exits.

BLUE FAIRY
Before I go, I just want a word with you, little cricket.

CRICKET
Me? I haven't been telling lies.

BLUE FAIRY
No, but you've been watching out for Pinocchio very nicely. Will you keep doing that?

CRICKET
Sure, I guess I've gotten fond of the little troublemaker.

BLUE FAIRY
Good. *(starts to leave, then turns back)* But, little cricket, try not to be such a nag, all right?

Blue Fairy exits.

GEPPETTO
Let's go home, Pinocchio.

NICE PINOCCHIO
Yes, Father.

CRICKET
Wait, aren't you going to scold him for being so naughty?

NICE PINOCCHIO
You're nagging again!

CRICKET
Oh right. Sorry.

GEPPETTO
Anyway, I can't scold Pinocchio. I'm too glad just to have him back.

During the song, the Cricket, Geppetto and Nice Pinocchio "walk." The tree gets moved off (with Naughty Pinocchio).

THE ADVENTURES OF PINOCCHIO

Music 06: Oh My Pinocchio (Same Arrangement As Music 03)
Vocal Chorus

GEPPETTO
Oh my Pinocchio,
That name does please me so!
You mean the world to me,
We'll be a family.

NICE PINOCCHIO
Call me Pinocchio,
That name does please me so!

CRICKET
More than a puppet now,
Why don't you take a bow?

GEPPETTO, NICE PINOCCHIO, CRICKET
See how you (I) walk around,
See how you (I) run and bound
No strings to tie you down!
Yes, you're (I'm) Pinocchio!

GEPPETTO
I must leave you, Pinocchio. I'm going fishing to catch us some dinner.

CRICKET
I'll make sure Pinocchio goes to school. Maybe he can share books with another student.

NICE PINOCCHIO
Goodbye, Father. I will be good, I promise.

Geppetto exits.

CRICKET
Come on, Pinocchio. The school is right over here.

NICE PINOCCHIO
Look, here come the townspeople again.

The Townsfolk enter, now including the COACH DRIVER, LAMPWICK and the UNRULY KIDS.

They bring on a coach (with Naughty Pinocchio behind it.)

Music 07: Village Parade (Same Arrangement As Music 02)
Vocal chorus, Instrumental dance

TOWNSFOLK
We're happy in our village,
Oh so happy all the time!
The sun shines all day in our village,
To be sad would be a crime!

The Townsfolk speak over the dance music.

CHEESEMAKER
Our village is so wonderful!

BAKER
The houses are so pretty!

OLIVE GROWER
The town hall is so tall!

TAILOR
The park is so green!

SHOEMAKER
The people are so friendly!

HATMAKER
Even the pets are friendly!

ALL TOWNSFOLK
Life is so happy here!

Townsfolk exit. Nice Pinocchio ends up with the Coach Driver, Lampwick and Unruly Kids.

COACH DRIVER
Hello there! Aren't you a fine-looking boy?

NICE PINOCCHIO
I'm not a real boy. Not yet, anyway.

CRICKET
Come on, Pinocchio, you need to go to school.

LAMPWICK
School? Only losers go to boring old school!

UNRULY KIDS
Yah! We never go to school!

NICE PINOCCHIO
What do you do instead?

LAMPWICK
We're going to this great place called Fun Land.

UNRULY KIDS
Yah! Fun Land!

> *Music 08 Fun Land 1 (Same Arrangement as Music 09)*
> *Tune: Funiculì, Funiculà (Denza and Turco, 1880)*
> *Vocal Chorus*

LAMPWICK, UNRULY KIDS
Fun Land, Fun Land,

LAMPWICK
Never go to school!

LAMPWICK, UNRULY KIDS
Fun Land, Fun Land,

LAMPWICK
All the kids are cool!

LAMPWICK, UNRULY KIDS
Where there's no work or any chores,
We play inside or out of doors!

COACH DRIVER
Come, don't be a fool!

LAMPWICK, UNRULY KIDS
And then we'll never go to school! Yah!

NICE PINOCCHIO
Wow! I want to go to Fun Land!

CRICKET
No, Pinocchio, good boys go to school.

COACH DRIVER
Would you like to go with us, my fine fellow?

NICE PINOCCHIO
Yes! My father said I can do whatever I want! Oh! Oh! Oh!

CRICKET
Not this again! Another lie!

SFX: Nose Growing Music

Nice Pinocchio holds his hands over his nose and staggers behind the wagon. Naughty Pinocchio emerges from the other side with his hands over his nose.

NAUGHTY PINOCCHIO
Oh! Oh! Oh!

When he takes his hands down, we can see his long nose.

CRICKET
Pinocchio! The fairies said this was your last chance!

NAUGHTY PINOCCHIO
I don't care! I like being naughty!

UNRULY KIDS
Yah! Being naughty is fun!

LAMPWICK
I like your nose like that. It's totally cool.

NAUGHTY PINOCCHIO
So leave me alone, Cricket! I'm going to Fun Land!

UNRULY KIDS
Yah!

Music 09: Fun Land 2 (Same arrangement as Music 08)
Vocal Chorus

The Cricket exits sadly.

During the song, the Coach Driver leads the wagon across the stage; Naughty Pinocchio, Lampwick and the Unruly Kids follow.

NAUGHTY PINOCCHIO, LAMPWICK, UNRULY KIDS
Fun Land, Fun Land,

NAUGHTY PINOCCHIO, LAMPWICK
Never go to school!

NAUGHTY PINOCCHIO, LAMPWICK, UNRULY KIDS
Fun Land, Fun Land,

NAUGHTY PINOCCHIO, LAMPWICK
All the kids are cool!

NAUGHTY PINOCCHIO, LAMPWICK, UNRULY KIDS
Where there's no work or any chores,
We play inside or out of doors!

COACH DRIVER
Come, don't be a fool!

NAUGHTY PINOCCHIO, LAMPWICK, UNRULY KIDS
And then we'll never go to school! Yah!

LAMPWICK
This is great! No more homework or—hee haw!

One of the Unruly Kids slips a pair of donkey ears on Lampwick. The wagon stops.

NAUGHTY PINOCCHIO
What is happening?

UNRULY KID 1
He's turning into a—Hee-haw!

As each Unruly Kid says "hee-haw," someone slips a pair of donkey ears on their head.

UNRULY KID 2
Look at you! Now you're a—Hee-haw!

UNRULY KID 3
Everybody's turning into a—Hee-haw!

OTHER UNRULY KIDS
Hey! Hey! Hee-haw!

By now, Lampwick and all the Unruly Kids have ears and can't say anything except "hee-haw."

LAMPWICK, UNRULY KIDS
(obviously trying to talk but unable to)
Hee-haw! Hee-haw! Hee-haw!

NAUGHTY PINOCCHIO
Why is everyone turning into a—Hee-haw!

Naughty Pinocchio claps his hand over his mouth. One of the Unruly Kids slips a pair of donkey ears on him.

COACH DRIVER
What a fine crop of mules I have here! Lazy selfish kids who won't go to school!

NAUGHTY PINOCCHIO
I'm not a—Hee-haw!

COACH DRIVER
You sound like a mule to me, kid.

NAUGHTY PINOCCHIO
I can still talk! Hee-haw! Well, I can still sort of talk. Hee-haw!

COACH DRIVER
Hmm, I guess you're just half a mule. Get lost, kid, I'm taking these mules to the market to sell.

> **Music 10: Fun Land 3/Hee-Haw**
> **Vocal Chorus with Hee-Haws**

The Coach Driver drives the mules across the stage.

LAMPWICK, UNRULY KIDS
Hee-haw, Hee-haw

COACH DRIVER
Acting like a fool!

LAMPWICK, UNRULY KIDS
Hee-haw, Hee-haw

COACH DRIVER
Turns you to a mule.

LAMPWICK, UNRULY KIDS
Hee-haw, Hee-haw
Hee-haw, Hee-haw!

COACH DRIVER
Come, my little mules
And now you'll never go to school! Yah!

They exit, leaving Naughty Pinocchio alone.

NAUGHTY PINOCCHIO
I don't want to be half a—Hee-haw! I want to be a real boy!

The Cricket enters.

CRICKET
Oh, Pinocchio, look what you've done now! I don't think even the Blue Fairy can fix that.

NAUGHTY PINOCCHIO
I will be good! I will be—Hee-haw!

CRICKET
I don't want to say I told you so—

NAUGHTY PINOCCHIO
Then don't say it!

CRICKET
Ok, let's just sit down here on the beach and wait for Geppetto to come home from fishing.

NAUGHTY PINOCCHIO
(pointing at where the whale will appear)
What's that? It looks like a—Hee-haw!

CRICKET
It's a whale!

> *The WHALE (a group of kids carrying something like a Chinese parade dragon) slowly crosses the stage. If desired, have any extra kids hold up a blue cloth as the water.*

Music 11 Song Of The Whale 1
Tune: O Sole Mio (Capurro, di Capua and Mazzucchi, 1898)
Whale sings verse, Geppetto sings chorus

WHALE VOICES
Keep swimming slowly
Through the deep blue waters,
Until I find some fish,
Until I get my wish.
Keep swimming slowly
Through the deep blue waters,
Until I find someone
To swallow whole.

> *At center, the Whale turns down and opens its mouth, so we see Geppetto just in time for him to sing.*

GEPPETTO
Save me, Pinocchio!
I'm in the whale!
I went out fishing,
Up came a gale.
Tomorrow will be too late,
Save me, Pinocchio
From this sad fate!

> *The Whale slowly exits.*

CRICKET
It's your father! We need to save him!

NAUGHTY PINOCCHIO
There's nothing I can do. Hee-haw!

CRICKET
Think! Think! There must be something.

> *The Cricket nudges Naughty Pinocchio, who just sits there. In desperation, the Cricket runs around the stage calling.*

CRICKET
Blue Fairy! Help us, please! Fairies-in-Training, we need you!

> *The Blue Fairy enters, followed by the Fairies in Training.*

BLUE FAIRY
We have been watching you, Pinocchio.

PINK FAIRY
We're very disappointed.

PURPLE FAIRY
We brought you to life so you could make Geppetto happy.

SILVER FAIRY
And so far, you've done a lousy job.

OTHER FAIRIES
(to Silver)
Ssh!

> *Naughty Pinocchio hangs his head in shame.*

SILVER FAIRY
Well, it's true! And if he keeps up like this, we'll never get our stars!

OTHER FAIRIES
Ssh!

CRICKET
Please, fairies, give Pinocchio another chance!

BLUE FAIRY
Pinocchio, do you want to stay as you are and be naughty, or be more like this…

The Blue Fairy waves her wand.

SFX: Fairy Magic (Loud)

Nice Pinocchio enters behind a rolling "mirror" frame. Naughty Pinocchio stands opposite the frame. Throughout this scene, the Pinocchios "reflect" each other.

NAUGHTY PINOCCHIO
Is that—Hee-haw—me?

BLUE FAIRY
That's you, when you are being good.

CRICKET
Yep, no long nose, no mule ears. That's you all right.

PINK FAIRY
You are so cute when you are good!

PURPLE FAIRY
Yes, it's too bad you didn't stay that way.

NAUGHTY PINOCCHIO
(gesturing with his reflection)
Look at me! I can wave…
and dance…
and wiggle…
and—Hee-haw!

SILVER FAIRY
You'll notice that the <u>good</u> puppet doesn't say Hee-haw.

NAUGHTY PINOCCHIO
I want to be like that again! Hee-haw!

BLUE FAIRY
You can be like that again if you try. But you have to show how much you want it.

The Blue Fairy waves her wand and Nice Pinocchio exits with the mirror.

SFX: Fairy Magic (Loud)

CRICKET
The first thing you need to do is help your father. Think, Pinocchio, think!

Naughty Pinocchio puts his head in his hands to think.

NAUGHTY PINOCCHIO
How can I save my father? How, how, hee-haw?

PINK FAIRY
I don't have any ideas.

PURPLE FAIRY
Me neither.

SILVER FAIRY
I don't even have a smart remark to make.

The Whale slowly enters.

Music 12: Song of the Whale 2
Whale sings verse

WHALE VOICES
Keep swimming slowly
Through the deep blue waters,
Until I find some fish,
Until I get my wish.
Keep swimming slowly
Through the deep blue waters,
Until I find someone
To swallow whole.

BLUE FAIRY
There's the whale, Pinocchio.

NAUGHTY PINOCCHIO
Wait! I have it! What if the whale sneezed?

CRICKET
He would blow Geppetto out of the water!

PINK FAIRY
Are you going to swim out there and tickle the whale?

PURPLE FAIRY
Spray the whale with pepper?

SILVER FAIRY
Do you think whales have hay fever?

NAUGHTY PINOCCHIO
Fairies, remember when you tried to shrink my nose?

CRICKET
It didn't work.

NAUGHTY PINOCCHIO
But it made me sneeze! Hee-haw! You could do the same thing to the whale!

BLUE FAIRY
That's a good idea, sisters.

PINK FAIRY
It would make Geppetto very happy!

PURPLE FAIRY
Maybe it's good enough to make Pinocchio a real boy!

SILVER FAIRY
And we could get our stars!

FAIRIES IN TRAINING
One, two, three!

The Fairies wave their wands together.

SFX: Fairy Magic & Whale Sneezing Music

WHALE VOICES
Ah-ah-ah-ah—

The Whale wheezes.

WHALE VOICES
CHOO!

Finally, the Whale sneezes and Geppetto comes flying downstage. Naughty Pinocchio and Cricket rush to his side. The Whale exits.

GEPPETTO
Pinocchio! You saved me!

NAUGHTY PINOCCHIO
I would do anything for you, Father, but it was really the fairies who saved you. Hee-haw!

CRICKET
Good for you, Pinocchio! You didn't tell a lie!

BLUE FAIRY
Yes, that's a good sign, little puppet.

NAUGHTY PINOCCHIO
Hee-haw!

GEPPETTO
Hee-haw? What happened to you?

NAUGHTY PINOCCHIO
I was bad. Hee-haw! I'm not good enough to be your son.

GEPPETTO
Yes you are!

NAUGHTY PINOCCHIO
I better go to market with the other—hee-haw—mules. Then you can have the money from selling me.

Naughty Pinocchio starts to exit. The Blue Fairy stops him.

BLUE FAIRY
Wait, little puppet. You have proven yourself to be a good son.

NAUGHTY PINOCCHIO
I have?

CRICKET, GEPPETTO
He has?

BLUE FAIRY
Yes, you took responsibility for your own mistakes.

NAUGHTY PINOCCHIO
I did?

CRICKET, GEPPETTO
Yes, you did!

BLUE FAIRY
I'll need your help for this one, sisters.

FAIRIES IN TRAINING
One, two, three!

All the fairies wave their wands.

SFX: Fairy Magic (Special)

Naughty Pinocchio staggers offstage. Nice Pinocchio enters with his hands over his nose. He has removed any "puppet" indicators like knee joints, round pink cheeks, etc. He is now a real boy.

NICE PINOCCHIO
Oh! Oh! Oh!

When he takes his hands down, we can see his short nose.

CRICKET
Pinocchio! You don't look like a puppet anymore!

NICE PINOCCHIO
Look at me! I'm a real boy!

GEPPETTO
Pinocchio!

NICE PINOCCHIO
Father!

GEPPETTO
Now I am truly happy!

Geppetto and Nice Pinocchio hug while the Cricket dances around them. The Fairies in Training look expectantly at the Blue Fairy.

BLUE FAIRY
Well, sisters, you know what that means!

The Blue Fairy waves her wand.

SFX: Fairy Magic (Special)

One by one, the Fairies in Training turn on the lights in their wands.

PINK FAIRY
Oh! My star!

PURPLE FAIRY
Oh! Now we are real fairies!

SILVER FAIRY
Oh! We totally deserve this!

Music 13: Song Of The Fairies 2
Vocal chorus

FAIRY GRADUATES
See us flutter
See us flitter
See our magic
Make us glitter!

ADD BLUE
Magic wands in
All their glory.
Now, we're off to go
Fix up some other story!

BLUE FAIRY
I'm so proud of you, sisters!

CRICKET
Sounds like a happy ending to me!

NICE PINOCCHIO
I'm certainly happy!

GEPPETTO
And now I really belong in this village, because I'm happy too!

Music 14: Village Parade Finale
Vocal chorus, dance break, vocal chorus

GEPPETTO, NICE PINOCCHIO, CRICKET
We're happy in our village,
Oh so happy all the time!
The sun shines all day in our village,
To be sad would be a crime!

*Instrumental music while
townsfolk enter.*

ALL
We're happy in our village,
Oh so happy all the time!
The sun shines all day in our village,
To be sad would be a crime!

THE END

THE ADVENTURES OF TOMMIE SAWYER
Loosely based on *The Adventures of Tom Sawyer* by Mark Twain

CHARACTERS

Roles marked with (M) or (F) should be cast accordingly; other roles are open M/F. Old Tommie, who can be either male or female, is played by the same actor throughout the show. Young Tommie is played by a different actor in each story. Ideally, Old Tommie and the Young Tommies should be the same gender, but it's not essential.

Opening	Fence	School	Treasure	Closing
Old Tommie	Old Tommie	Old Tommie	Old Tommie	Old Tommie
	Cousin Sid	Scout	Young Tommie 3	
	Aunt Polly (F)	Teacher	Huck (M)	
	Cousin Mary (F)	Amy (F)	Jo	
	Young Tommie 1	Drew	Becky (F)	
	Huck (M)	Becky (F)	Cousin Emily (F)	
	Bennie	Donnie	Cousin Tracy	
	Jo	Young Tommie 2	Cousin Lee	
		Frankie	Becky's Father (M)	
Ensemble 1	Gullible Kid 1	Jamie	Becky's Mother (F)	
Ensemble 2	Gullible Kid 2	Sandy	Ensemble 4	Ensemble 6
Ensemble 3	Gullible Kid 3	Mayor	Ensemble 5	Ensemble 7

Minimum: 12 (2 M, 5 F, 5 M or F). This assumes that everyone is in every story, doubling as needed.

Maximum for everyone to have at least one line: 41 (3 M, 7 F, 31 M or F)

For a small cast, use the same Huck, Becky and Jo in two stories each. However, more cast members can have lines if you use a new actor each time.

The entire cast is onstage throughout the show.

SET

A modern-day playground with a park bench and prop box. There is a wooden fence, either as a set piece or part of the permanent set. (The fence could be as simple as a sheet of cardboard held by cast members). The school, cave, etc. are all imagined rather than physical sets. The simple costume pieces and props come from the prop box.

LENGTH

30 minutes (2 stories)/40 minutes (3 stories)

STRUCTURE

	Songs
Opening	When Tommie Tells Stories A *(When Johnny Comes Marching Home)*
How I Painted the Fence	It's So Fun to Paint the Fence *(If You've Only Got a Moustache, Stephen Foster)*
How I Closed the School	School Days *(School Days, Cobb & Edwards)*
How I Found the Treasure	Pirate Island *(Arkansas Traveler, Faulkner)*
Closing	Closing: When Tommie Tells Stories B

The Opening, Story 1 and Closing form the heart of the show. To keep under half an hour, do only Story 2 OR 3 (3 is slightly longer than the others). Each story contains its own transition into the action.

Opening: Old Tommie's Stories

A modern-day playground with a park bench and prop box. There is a wooden fence, either as a movable set piece or part of the permanent set.

> **Music 01: When Tommie Tells Stories A**
> **Tune: When Johnny Comes Marching Home (Lambert, 1863)**
> **Instrumental chorus, two vocal choruses**

ENSEMBLE MEMBERS (except Old Tommie) enter during the instrumental chorus playing hopscotch and other classic playground games.

ENSEMBLE MEMBERS (NO OLD TOMMIE)
When Tommie tells stories, we all cheer
Hurrah! Hurrah!
Old Tommie has tales we love to hear
Hurrah! Hurrah!
At first we'll cheer, and then we'll shout,
As Tommie brings all the mischief out.
And we'll sing and play
When Tommie starts telling tales!

During the second vocal chorus, some Ensemble Members escort OLD TOMMIE onstage. He/she is very old and hobbles over to sit on the park bench.

ENSEMBLE MEMBERS
When Tommie tells stories, we all cheer
Hurrah! Hurrah!
Old Tommie has tales we love to hear
Hurrah! Hurrah!
At first we'll cheer, and then we'll shout,
As Tommie brings all the mischief out.
And we'll sing and play
When Tommie starts telling tales!

Once Old Tommie is seated, the Ensemble Members sit on the floor around the bench.

OLD TOMMIE
Ah! How I love to sit down after a long walk!

ENSEMBLE MEMBERS
Yay! Old Tommie!

OLD TOMMIE
And how I love to have all these bright young faces gathered around me!

ENSEMBLE 1
Please tell us a story, Tommie!

ENSEMBLE 2
We love your stories!

ENSEMBLE 3
All about being a kid in the olden days!

ENSEMBLE MEMBERS
Please, Tommie!

OLD TOMMIE
You really like my stories, eh?

ENSEMBLE MEMBERS
Yes! Yes! Yes!

OLD TOMMIE
Well, all righty then.

*CONTINUE WITH
STORY 1*

THE ADVENTURES OF TOMMIE SAWYER

Story 1: How I Painted the Fence

ENSEMBLE MEMBERS
Yay! A story!

OLD TOMMIE
Did I ever tell you about the time I painted the fence?

A FEW ENSEMBLE MEMBERS
We love that story!

ENSEMBLE MEMBER (SID)
Painting a fence? That sound really boring.

A FEW ENSEMBLE MEMBERS
(to the Ensemble Member who will play Sid, ad lib)
Ssh! Be quiet! Don't be so rude! We want to hear!

OLD TOMMIE
(rambling a bit)
Now this is a special story, one of my favorites, about back when I was just a kid…

ENSEMBLE MEMBER (SID)
(interrupting)
C'mon, get on with painting the fence already!

OLD TOMMIE
(to Sid, sharply)
Listen you, I am one hundred and eighty-seven years old, and I don't need some young whippersnapper teachin' me how to tell stories. So just button your lip!

A FEW ENSEMBLE MEMBERS
(to Sid, ad lib)
So there! Old Tommie is the best! Let Old Tommie talk!

OLD TOMMIE
Where was I? Oh yes, back then I lived with my dear aunt…

ENSEMBLE MEMBERS
Aunt Polly!

Old Tommie hands an apron to a girl who will play AUNT POLLY.

OLD TOMMIE
She was always callin' for me.

AUNT POLLY
(calling in different directions)
Tommie! Tommie Sawyer!

OLD TOMMIE
There was also my sweet cousin...

ENSEMBLE MEMBERS
Cousin Mary!

> *Old Tommie hands a hair bow to a girl to play COUSIN MARY.*

COUSIN MARY
(calling)
Come home, Tommie! Breakfast is ready!

AUNT POLLY
(calling)
Yoo-hoo! Tommie!

OLD TOMMIE
I had another cousin, not so sweet...

ENSEMBLE MEMBERS
Cousin Sid!

OLD TOMMIE
And I know just the right person to play Sid for us! You!

> *Old Tommie hands a beanie to the rude Ensemble Member to play COUSIN SID.*

COUSIN SID
(calling)
Tommie! You're in trouble! Nyah-nyah-nyah-nyah!

COUSIN MARY
(to Sid)
Sid, be nice now!
(calling)
Come home, Tommie!

COUSIN SID
(calling)
Tommie! Nyah-nyah-nyah-nyah!

AUNT POLLY
(to Sid)
That's enough, Sid!
(calling)
Yoo-hoo! Tommie!

OLD TOMMIE
I took my time, but I always came home eventually.

ENSEMBLE MEMBERS
Where's Tommie?

> *Old Tommie gestures to an Ensemble Member to play YOUNG TOMMIE 1. He/she stands up and comes over to the park bench and receives a straw hat.*

OLD TOMMIE
(to Young Tommie 1)
Now remember, I was never a bad kid, just full of mischief.

YOUNG TOMMIE 1
Yes, Old Tommie.

OLD TOMMIE
(to Young Tommie 1)
Now get in there and be Tommie!

> *Old Tommie gives Young Tommie 1 a push. He/she runs over to Aunt Polly.*

YOUNG TOMMIE 1
Here I am, Aunt Polly!

AUNT POLLY
And where have you been?

COUSIN SID
Tommie was out fishin' with Huck Finn!

YOUNG TOMMIE 1
Sure I was. What's wrong with that?

COUSIN MARY
Huck Finn, that wild boy? Oh Tommie, I wish you wouldn't.

COUSIN SID
Tommie played hooky from school yesterday to go fishin' with Huck!

YOUNG TOMMIE 1
(trying to shush Sid)
You hush up!

AUNT POLLY
Playing hooky! Is that true?

COUSIN SID
I saw it with my own eyes!

YOUNG TOMMIE 1
(trying to shush Sid)
You hush up!

COUSIN MARY
Hush Sid, it's not nice to be a tattletale.

AUNT POLLY
Tommie! Answer me! Did you play hooky from school?

YOUNG TOMMIE 1
(mumbling)
Yes I did, Aunt Polly.
(bursting out)
But there's nothin' wrong with Huck Finn! He just ain't got a family to look after him!

AUNT POLLY
Well now, that's a sad thing for him, but it's no excuse for your missing school. I reckon you'll have to work all morning to make up for it.

YOUNG TOMMIE 1
Work? On a Saturday?

AUNT POLLY
On a Saturday.

COUSIN MARY
Without breakfast?

AUNT POLLY
Without breakfast.

COUSIN SID
Tommie has to wo-ork! Tommie has to wo-ork!

YOUNG TOMMIE 1
You hush up!

AUNT POLLY
The fence needs painting. You do that, and THEN you can have something to eat.

> *Ensemble members bring on a board "fence" (unless the fence is in the permanent set).*

YOUNG TOMMIE 1
Oh, Aunt Polly, do I gotta?

> *Aunt Polly gets a paint can and brush from the prop box and sternly holds them out to Young Tommie 1..*

AUNT POLLY
Indeed you do. Now get to work.

> *Aunt Polly exits or sits down.*

COUSIN SID
Tommie has to wo-ork! Tommie has to wo-ork!

COUSIN MARY
Sid, be nice now! I'm awfully sorry, Tommie!

> *Cousin Mary takes Sid by the arm and drags him/her away. As they go, Sid keeps taunting Young Tommie.*

COUSIN SID
Tommie has to wo-ork! Tommie has to wo-ork!

Young Tommie sticks his/her tongue out at Sid, then turns to the fence.

YOUNG TOMMIE 1
This old fence must be a mile long! I could be paintin' for days and days.

Young Tommie makes a few half-hearted efforts at painting the fence.

OLD TOMMIE
I was feelin' pretty gloomy, all right, and the worst thought was that soon some kids would come along and make fun of me for havin' to work. The very thought of that…

OLD TOMMIE, YOUNG TOMMIE 1
(together)
…burnt me like fire!

Young Tommie 1 paints the fence a little more, very sloppily.

Old Tommie points at a boy Ensemble Member to be HUCK FINN. Huck grabs a bandanna and fishing pole and walks over to see what Young Tommie is doing.

HUCK FINN
Whatcha doin', Tommie? I thought we was gonna go fishin' some more.

YOUNG TOMMIE 1
Oh Huck, you and your fishin' got me into heaps of trouble and now I gotta paint this darn fence.

HUCK FINN
Whew! That's a lot of fence to paint! You're gonna be workin' for hours!

YOUNG TOMMIE 1
(bitterly)
Yep.

HUCK FINN
You ain't gonna have no fun the whole day!

YOUNG TOMMIE 1
(even more bitterly)
Nope.

HUCK FINN
If you was free like me, you could be out catchin' a heap of fish. They're bitin' like crazy right now.

YOUNG TOMMIE 1
(bursting out)
I know, I know! Don't talk about it no more!

HUCK FINN
Ohhhhhh. Sorry, Tommie. I reckon I better leave you to it.

YOUNG TOMMIE 1
Fine. Go back to your fishin'.

> *Young Tommie turns reluctantly back to painting. Huck exits or sits down.*
>
> *Old Tommie gives an apple to an Ensemble Member to be BENNIE, but holds him/her back from entering the scene.*

YOUNG TOMMIE 1
(looking offstage)
Oh, here comes Bennie. He/she'll tease me like crazy for havin' to work.

OLD TOMMIE
Just then, an inspiration burst upon me! Nothin' less than the best idea I ever had!

YOUNG TOMMIE 1
(suddenly inspired)
What a great idea!

> *Young Tommie starts painting with evident enjoyment. Bennie enters, tossing the apple in the air and catching it. Young Tommie pays no attention, but goes on painting, whistling merrily. Bennie stops and sneers.*

BENNIE
Hello Tommie, you got to work, huh?

YOUNG TOMMIE 1
(turning in pretended surprise)
Why, it's you, Bennie!

BENNIE
(taunting)
I'm goin' swimmin'. Too bad you gotta work, or you could go too.

YOUNG TOMMIE 1
You call this work? All I know is, it suits me fine.

> *Young Tommie paints with enthusiasm. Bennie watches with growing interest.*

BENNIE
Say Tommie, let me paint a little.

> *Young Tommie considers, is about to consent; but then changes his/her mind.*

YOUNG TOMMIE 1
No, I reckon it won't do, Bennie. Aunt Polly says I'm the only one who can do it right. Sorry.

BENNIE
I'll give you my apple!

YOUNG TOMMIE 1
Aw gee, I'd like to, but I'm havin' too much fun!

BENNIE
I'll give you everythin' in my pockets!

OLD TOMMIE
Hehehe! All I had to do was make paintin' look like fun!

> *Both Tommies sing. Young Tommie 1 paints like it's the funnest thing in the world. Bennie keeps offering more and more goodies, until finally Young Tommie, ever so*

> *reluctantly, gives the brush to Bennie and takes the goodies.*

> **Music 02: It's So Fun to Paint the Fence A**
> **Tune: If You've Only Got a Moustache (Stephen Foster, 1864)**
> **One verse and chorus**

OLD TOMMIE, YOUNG TOMMIE 1
Oh! all of you bored boys and girls,
Don't ever give up in despair,
For there's always a chance while there's life
To have all the fun that you dare.
No matter what may be your age,
You always can show lots of sense,
For there isn't a game to compare
With the fun of painting the fence,
Paint the fence, paint the fence,
It's so fun to paint the fence!

> *Old Tommie points at an Ensemble Member to be JO.*
>
> *Jo enters. Bennie is painting away, while Young Tommie tries to look jealous.*

JO
Hi Tommie, what're you doin'?

YOUNG TOMMIE 1
Hi Jo! Just wishin' Bennie would get tired of paintin', so's I could get back at that fence.

BENNIE
(still painting)
Gosh, this is fun! You should try it, Jo!

JO
Can I, Tommie? Let me paint a while!

YOUNG TOMMIE 1
I do got an extra brush, but I hate to miss all the fun…

JO
Looky, Tommie, what if I give you all the stuff I've got in my pockets? Will you let me paint then? Please?

YOUNG TOMMIE 1
(making a big show of reluctance)
Well, all righty.

> *Young Tommie takes the goodies and gives the extra brush to Jo. Jo starts painting.*

Music 03: It's So Fun to Paint the Fence B
Verse, chorus, verse, chorus with ending

> *One by one, other GULLIBLE KIDS enter. They see what is happening and want to join in. They give Young Tommie their goodies; he gives them each a brush (or they bring their own) and they start painting.*

BENNIE, JO, ADD GULLIBLE KIDS ONE BY ONE
Oh! all of you bored boys and girls,
Don't ever give up in despair,
For there's always a chance while there's life
To have all the fun that you dare.
No matter what may be your age,
You always can show lots of sense,
For there isn't a game to compare
With the fun of painting the fence!

BENNIE, JO, GULLIBLE KIDS, OLD TOMMIE, YOUNG TOMMIE 1
Paint the fence, paint the fence,
It's so fun to paint the fence!

> *All the Gullible Kids are happily painting and singing. Young Tommie sits at ease and gloats over all his/her new goodies.*

ALL
Oh! all of you bored boys and girls,
Don't ever give up in despair,
For there's always a chance while there's life
To have all the fun that you dare.
No matter what may be your age,
You always can show lots of sense,

**For there isn't a game to compare
With the fun of painting the fence!
Paint the fence, paint the fence,
It's so fun to paint the fence!
Paint the fence, paint the fence,
It's so fun to paint the fence!**

GULLIBLE KID 1
All done, Tommie!

GULLIBLE KID 2
That's three coats of paint!

GULLIBLE KID 3
Looks mighty good to me!

GULLIBLE KIDS, BENNIE, JO
(ad lib)
That was fun! Shucks, I wish this fence was longer. Any more paintin' we could do for ya, Tommie?

YOUNG TOMMIE 1
(looking offstage)
Here comes Aunt Polly! Get lost, kids!

GULLIBLE KIDS, BENNIE, JO
(ad lib)
Thanks, Tommie! I sure liked that! Lemme know next time you gotta paint! Bye now!

The Gullible Kids, Bennie and Jo scatter and sit down. Young Tommie grabs a brush and pretends to be finishing up, exhausted.

Aunt Polly enters, followed by Cousin Mary and Cousin Sid.

AUNT POLLY
Tommie, I came out to apologize. I was too hard on you, making you go without breakfast.

COUSIN SID
Nyah-nyah, I ate it for you!

COUSIN MARY
I baked you some cookies to make up for it.

AUNT POLLY
Tommie, come on in and take a break.

YOUNG TOMMIE 1
I don't need a break, Aunt Polly. I'm all done!

AUNT POLLY, COUSIN MARY, COUSIN SID
What?!?

Aunt Polly, Cousin Mary and Cousin Sid stare at the fence in wonder.

YOUNG TOMMIE 1
Yep, it's all done. Three coats!

COUSIN MARY
That looks wonderful, Tommie!

COUSIN SID
I don't believe it. You musta cheated somehow.

AUNT POLLY
(to Sid)
Sid, you hush up.
(to Young Tommie)
Tommie, I'm proud of you. Come on in and rest a while.

YOUNG TOMMIE 1
(pitifully tired)
I will, Aunt Polly. As soon as I clean the brushes.

AUNT POLLY
Aw now, you've worked hard enough for one day.
(to Sid)
Sid, you go clean the brushes.

COUSIN SID
Huh? Why me?

AUNT POLLY
Because Tommie deserves to come inside and have some cookies. Don't you, Tommie?

Cousin Sid sulkily takes the brushes and cans. Young Tommie sticks his/her tongue out at Sid.

COUSIN MARY
See Tommie, doesn't it feel good to have a job well done?

YOUNG TOMMIE 1
Yes it does! It feels real good!

Aunt Polly and Cousin Mary put their arms around Young Tommie and start walking him/her into the house. Young Tommie breaks away and comes to stand next to Old Tommie by the end of the next speech.

OLD TOMMIE
Hehehe! That was the funnest paintin' job I ever done! And I gotta bunch of goodies too!

YOUNG TOMMIE 1
And Sid has to clean the brushes!

OLD TOMMIE
Hehehe! That was the best part!

Old Tommie and Young Tommie stick their tongues out at Sid.

OLD TOMMIE
(continued)
So kids, now you know the story of "How I—

ALL
"Painted the Fence!" Yay!

Old Tommie shakes hands with Young Tommie as everybody sings.

During the song, Ensemble Members "show off" the fence by rolling it around and off.)

Music 04: It's So Fun to Paint the Fence C
One verse and chorus with ending

ALL
Oh! all of you bored boys and girls,
Don't ever give up in despair,
For there's always a chance while there's life
To have all the fun that you dare.
No matter what may be your age,
You always can show lots of sense,
For there isn't a game to compare
With the fun of painting the fence!
Paint the fence, paint the fence,
It's so fun to paint the fence!
Paint the fence, paint the fence,
It's so fun to paint the fence!

CONTINUE WITH
STORY 2 OR 3 OR THE
CLOSING

Story 2: How I Closed the School

> *The Ensemble Members are seated around Old Tommie, as in the Opening.*

OLD TOMMIE
So did I ever tell you about the time I closed the school?

A FEW ENSEMBLE MEMBERS
Closed it forever?

OLD TOMMIE
(chuckling)
Not forever, just for a few glorious hours.

ENSEMBLE MEMBER (SCOUT)
So you didn't like school? Maybe you just weren't smart enough, huh?

OLD TOMMIE
(sharply)
No, I knew all the answers, but I just didn't like bein' questioned.
(pointedly)
And I still don't like it.

> *Old Tommie shoots a dirty look at the Ensemble Member who will play Scout.*

ENSEMBLE MEMBERS
Tell us the story! Tell us!

OLD TOMMIE
Well now, to lead the class we had a...

ENSEMBLE MEMBERS
Teacher!

> *Old Tommie points at an Ensemble Member to play TEACHER. He/she gets a pointer from the prop box, then moves to the front of the class.*

OLD TOMMIE
And there were a lot of kids—like Becky and Amy and Drew, Jamie, Sandy, Frankie, Donnie…

> *Old Tommie points at Ensemble Members to play SCHOOLKIDS. They stand up and move to face Teacher as if they are in class. Girls put on hair bows or pinafores.*
>
> NOTE: *If desired, add Mary and kids from the previous story (except Huck, who does not go to school). Don't use the Mayor yet.*

OLD TOMMIE
And there was Scout, a kid who reminded me a lot of… you!

> *Old Tommie points at Scout, who puts on thick glasses and joins the class.*

OLD TOMMIE
We used to do whatever Teacher told us.

TEACHER
Now class, before we go to morning recess, let us practice our school song. Ready? Begin.

Music 05: School Days A
Tune: School Days (Cobb & Edwards, 1907)
One chorus

> *Teacher conducts the Kids.*

TEACHER, SCHOOLKIDS
School days, school days
Happy, ordered school days
Reading and 'riting and 'rithmetic
Taught ev'ryday so they're sure to stick.
Monday we study history,
Tuesday we learn geography,
And on Friday we have a spelling bee!
We learn something new ev'ry day.

TEACHER
Very good. The Mayor will be mighty impressed when he/she arrives to give out the prize.

SCHOOLKIDS
What is the prize?

Teacher pulls a magnifying glass from the prop box.

TEACHER
This fine magnifying glass!

SCHOOLKIDS
Ooh!

TEACHER
Now, it's time for morning recess.

SCHOOLKIDS
Yay!

Teacher moves upstage. The Kids scatter. Group 1: AMY, DREW, DONNIE and BECKY; Group 2: FRANKIE and JAMIE; Group 3: SCOUT, SANDY and any extra kids. Groups 2 and 3 cluster together in inaudible games. Group 1 takes focus.

AMY
So Becky, how do you like our school?

DREW
Is it as good as your old school?

BECKY
I dunno. I only been here an hour.

DONNIE
You're lucky to start on a Prize Day.

BECKY
Oh, was that what Teacher was talkin' about?

DREW
Yep! The Mayor will be here!

AMY
And whoever has the most yellow tickets wins a prize!

> *Amy, Donnie and Drew each show off a handful of yellow tickets.*

BECKY
What're those for?

AMY
We get 'em for answerin' Teacher's questions about nature.

DONNIE
You know, like bugs and trees. Teacher really likes stuff like that.

DREW
See how many tickets I got?

AMY
I'm gonna see how many Scout has! He/she is the smartest!

> *Amy runs off to join Group 3. Becky, Donnie and Drew fade to one side while Group 2 comes forward.*

OLD TOMMIE
Yep, those yellow tickets were the big thing that day. Too bad I didn't have any—yet.

> *Old Tommie gestures to an Ensemble Member who will play Young Tommie 2. He/she stands up and comes over to the park bench, where he/she receives the same straw hat as Young Tommie 1.*

OLD TOMMIE
(to Young Tommie 2)
Get on in there and get us some tickets!

YOUNG TOMMIE 2
Yes, Old Tommie.

*Old Tommie gives Young
Tommie a push. He/she joins
Group 2 (Frankie/Jamie).*

YOUNG TOMMIE 2
Hey kids!

FRANKIE
You're late!

JAMIE
Like always!

YOUNG TOMMIE 2
Have they gave out the prize yet? Who got it?

FRANKIE
Not yet. I'm not gonna win, becuz I only got two tickets.

*Frankie and Jamie each show
off their yellow tickets.*

JAMIE
I only got three.

YOUNG TOMMIE 2
If you ain't gonna win, why don't you swap me for your tickets? I can give you each... lemme see...

*Young Tommie rifles his/her
pockets and brings out some of
the goodies from the Fence scene.*

FRANKIE
Ooh, I could sure use a new fishin' hook!

JAMIE
I always wanted a steelie marble like that one!

YOUNG TOMMIE 2
All righty then, hand over the tickets. Here's your stuff...

*Young Tommie, Frankie and
Jamie huddle together as they*

make their swap. Focus shifts to Group 3, where Scout is showing off a huge batch of tickets to Amy, Sandy and any extra kids.

SCOUT
(smugly)
And I got this twelfth one for knowing what kind of butterflies like milkweed plants.

SANDY
Ooh, what kind is that?

SCOUT
Monarch butterflies, of course.

SANDY
Oh yeah, of course!

EXTRA SCHOOLKIDS
Of course!

AMY
Oh Scout, you are so stuck on yourself!

SANDY, EXTRA SCHOOLKIDS
You sure are!

Young Tommie moves to join Becky, Donnie and Drew.

YOUNG TOMMIE 2
Hey kids, wanna swap with me?

DONNIE
What'ya got?

DREW
Any good stuff?

YOUNG TOMMIE 2
Looky here!

Young Tommie holds out some of the goodies from his/her

> *pockets. Becky, Donnie and Drew huddle together to see.*

SCOUT
(pointing at the huddle)
What's goin' on over there?

SANDY, EXTRA SCHOOLKIDS
Let's go find out!

> *Sandy and any extra kids join the huddle around Tommie. Frankie and Jamie drift over to where Scout is counting his/her tickets to impress Amy.*

FRANKIE
Looky all those tickets!

JAMIE
Looks like you're gonna win, Scout.

SCOUT
Yes, it certainly does.

AMY
Scout always wins!

YOUNG TOMMIE 2
(from the huddle)
Okay kids, that's all your tickets.

> *The Schoolkids drift away from Tommie, except Becky.*

YOUNG TOMMIE 2
(to Becky)
You're new here, ain't ya? What's your name?

BECKY
Becky Thatcher. And you're Tommie, ain't ya?

YOUNG TOMMIE 2
Thomas/Thomasina Sawyer, at your service. Hey, would you like to be best friends?

BECKY
Gosh, that'd be nice.

YOUNG TOMMIE 2
Here, you just take one bite outta this apple…

> *Young Tommie holds out the apple from his/her pocket. Becky takes a bite.*

BECKY
Now what?

YOUNG TOMMIE 2
Now I take a bite, and that means we're gonna be best friends forever.

> *Young Tommie is about to take a bite when Amy rushes over.*

AMY
Tommie Sawyer! You can't do that with her!

YOUNG TOMMIE 2
Uh-oh.

BECKY
What's wrong?

AMY
You bit the apple with me just two days ago!

YOUNG TOMMIE 2
Yeah, but I like Becky now, an awful lot…

AMY
(crying)
You said we were gonna be best friends forever!

YOUNG TOMMIE 2
Oh Amy, don't go all crybaby!

AMY
Fine! I'm gonna be best friends with Scout instead!

> *Amy runs off to join Scout's group.*

BECKY
Gosh Tommie, I'm awful sorry to give you such a fuss.

YOUNG TOMMIE 2
Oh never mind her.
(defiantly biting the apple)
She always comes cryin' back.

> *Teacher rings a bell from the prop box. The Schoolkids reassemble in class formation. Young Tommie hands the apple to Old Tommie, then meanders into a place as far away from Scout and Amy as possible.*

TEACHER
Now children, I'm honored to introduce the Mayor…

> *Teacher gestures, but there's no one there. Old Tommie looks alarmed.*

OLD TOMMIE
Dad gum it, I forgot to call out a Mayor!
(pointing to an Ensemble Member)
You! Go be Mayor!

> *The MAYOR puts on a top hat and stands next to Teacher.*

MAYOR
Ahem! Good morning, boys and girls!

SCHOOLKIDS
Good mornin', Mayor!

MAYOR
(pompously)
I have taken time from my busy schedule to celebrate the superior knowledge some students have attained here in this worthy civic establishment…

> *The Schoolkids fidget in boredom. The Mayor could go on like this all day, but Teacher interrupts.*

TEACHER
(interrupting)
The class would like to sing the school song for you, Mayor.

MAYOR
(surprised at being stopped)
Oh! Very well.

Music 06: School Days B
One chorus

---

*Teacher conducts the Schoolkids
as the Mayor looks on.*

TEACHER, SCHOOLKIDS, YOUNG TOMMIE 2
School days, school days
Happy, ordered school days
Reading and 'riting and 'rithmetic
Taught ev'ryday so they're sure to stick.
Monday we study history,
Tuesday we learn geography,
And on Friday we have a spelling bee!
We learn something new ev'ry day.

Mayor applauds politely.

MAYOR
Congratulations on that entirely adequate performance, which reminds me of the upcoming election—

TEACHER
(interrupting)
That was very good, class.

MAYOR
(surprised at being stopped)
Oh! Very well.

TEACHER
Now, let's see who has the most yellow tickets… Scout?

*Teacher expects Scout to win, so
looks right at him/her.*

SCOUT
(with fake modesty)
Oh, I only have a few… twelve, I think.

AMY
No Scout, you have sixteen, remember?

Amy passes Scout her four tickets and smirks at Tommie.

SCOUT
Oh! Uh yes Teacher, I have sixteen.

TEACHER
Nobody could beat that! Please come up here, Scout. Mayor, will you do the honors?

Teacher hands the magnifying glass to the Mayor. Scout moves next to the Mayor. Young Tommie 2 frantically counts tickets.

MAYOR
I am proud to recognize this fine young representative of our fair city—

YOUNG TOMMIE 2
Wait! I got seventeen tickets!

There is a stunned reaction.

SCOUT
You? How?

AMY
I don't believe it!

MAYOR
(annoyed at being interrupted)
Well, come on up here then.

YOUNG TOMMIE 2
Here I come!

Young Tommie pushes Scout aside and stands by the Mayor.

MAYOR
(back to the speech)
I am proud to recognize this fine young representative—

SCOUT
Wait! This isn't fair!

MAYOR
(annoyed at being interrupted, to Scout)
Shush!
(back to the speech)
I am proud to recognize this fine—

TEACHER
You know, I don't remember ever giving Tommie a ticket...

MAYOR
(annoyed at being interrupted, to Teacher)
Never mind that!
(back to the speech)
I am proud to recognize—

AMY
Hey, if Tommie knows so much, ask him/her a question now!

FRANKIE, JAMIE, DONNIE, SANDY, DREW, EXTRA SCHOOLKIDS
(ad lib)
Yeah! Ask him/her a question! This'll be fun! Let's hear what Tommie has to say!

BECKY
Hey! Don't pick on Tommie! He/she's my friend!

YOUNG TOMMIE 2
That's okay, Becky.
(to Teacher)
Teacher, that's fine by me.

TEACHER
All right, let's see if you deserve the prize.
(to the Mayor)
If that's agreeable to you, your Honor.

MAYOR
Yes, yes, yes, just get it over with already so I can finish my speech!

SCOUT
(to Tommie)
If you get it wrong, I get the prize!

*Young Tommie 2 sticks his/her
tongue out at Scout.*

YOUNG TOMMIE 2
(to Scout)
Whiner!
(to Teacher)
Teacher, go ahead and shoot me a question.

TEACHER
Mmm, let me see… All right Tommie, what kind of animal sheds its skin?

YOUNG TOMMIE 2
Oh, I know the answer to that. In fact, I'll show ya!

> *Young Tommie pulls a snakeskin from his/her pocket and holds it up.*

YOUNG TOMMIE 2
See?
(acting suddenly puzzled)
Hey, this is just the skin. What happened to the snake?

TEACHER, MAYOR, SCHOOLKIDS
The snake?!?

YOUNG TOMMIE 2
(exaggeratedly searching the floor)
Yeah, the snake was in my pocket when I got here. It musta crawled out!

TEACHER
It's somewhere in the school!

MAYOR
A snake! Let me out of here!

SCHOOLKIDS
(ad lib)
Aah! I hate snakes! What if it slithers up my leg? I'm not stayin' in here! I'm gonna tell my Pappy! Only Tommie would bring a snake to school!

> *Pandemonium. Everyone (except Becky) runs screaming from the school, led by the Mayor. Young Tommie is left with Becky.*

BECKY
Shame on you Tommie, for bringin' a snake to school!

YOUNG TOMMIE 2
Not me! There never was no snake, just the skin!
(laughing)
I fooled them all and won the prize too!

*Young Tommie holds up the
magnifying glass. Becky gasps,
then laughs too.*

OLD TOMMIE
Hehehe! And that's how I closed the school!

Music 07: School Days C
One chorus plus ending

*Old and Young Tommie start
the song. Others join in
gradually. Old Tommie shakes
hands with Young Tommie.*

OLD TOMMIE, YOUNG TOMMIE 2
School days, school days
Happy, ordered school days

ADD BECKY
Reading and 'riting and 'rithmetic

ADD FRANKIE, DONNIE, DREW, JAMIE, SANDY
Taught ev'ryday so they're sure to stick.

ADD TEACHER, MAYOR
Monday we study history,

ADD AMY, SCOUT
Tuesday we learn geography,

ADD EXTRA SCHOOLKIDS
And on Friday we have a spelling bee!

ADD ALL
We learn something new ev'ry day.
We learn something new ev'ry day!

*CONTINUE WITH
STORY 3 OR THE
CLOSING*

Story 3: How I Found the Treasure

NOTE: This story has many places where the ensemble can interact (like holding up a blue cloth as water, or forming the cave entrance). Old Tommie directs Ensemble Members as needed.

> *The Ensemble Members are seated around Old Tommie, as in the Opening.*

OLD TOMMIE
Did I ever tell you about the time I found the treasure?

ENSEMBLE 4
What kind of treasure?

OLD TOMMIE
Why, pirate treasure, of course!

ENSEMBLE 5
You grew up near pirates?

OLD TOMMIE
Sure! Ain't you never heard about the Pirates of the Mississippi?

ENSEMBLE MEMBERS
No!

OLD TOMMIE
Yep, they raided along the river for years, gatherin' loot all the way from Ioway down to New Orleans.

ENSEMBLE MEMBERS
Ooh, really?

OLD TOMMIE
And they buried their treasure on Pirate Island.

ENSEMBLE MEMBERS
Tell us the story!

OLD TOMMIE
All righty then. It all started when me *(pointing)* and Huck Finn *(pointing)* and Jo *(pointing)* decided to run away

> *Old Tommie gestures to Ensemble Members to play YOUNG TOMMIE 3 (straw*

> hat), HUCK (bandanna) and
> JO (vest). They stand and meet
> near the prop box. As they talk,
> they each gather a shovel and a
> sack that can be slung over a
> shoulder.

YOUNG TOMMIE 3
C'mon kids, let's run away and hide on Pirate Island!

HUCK
Lotsa good fishin' over there.

JO
We can live like pirates!

YOUNG TOMMIE 3
We'll do more'n that—we'll dig up all their treasure!

HUCK, JO
Yay!

OLD TOMMIE
And so we "borrowed" a canoe and rowed over to the island.

> The runaways line up in an
> imaginary canoe and use their
> shovels as paddles to "row" to
> the island. If desired, Old
> Tommie points to Ensemble
> Members to hold up a blue cloth
> as the river. They sing as they
> row.

Music 08: Pirate Island A
Tune: Arkansas Traveler (Faulkner, 1800s)
Vocal chorus, instrumental interlude, vocal chorus

OLD TOMMIE, RUNAWAYS
Once there was an island stuffed with gold,
Hid by pirates raidin' on the river.
Buried all their gold to beat the law,
Ended up in prison down in Arkansas!

> During the instrumental
> interlude, Old Tommie and the

> *Runaways yell rhythmically over the music.*

OLD TOMMIE
There was gold! (RUNAWAYS: Ooh!)
There was silver! (Ah!)
There was rubies all glowin' and red! (Wow!)
There was pearls! (Ooh!)
There was diamonds! (Ah!)
There was em'ralds as big as your head! (Wow!)

ALL
Once there was an island stuffed with gold,
Hid by pirates raidin' on the river.
Buried all their gold to beat the law,
Ended up in prison down in Arkansas!

> *As the song ends, the runaways step out of the "canoe" and look around the island. They drop their sacks in a heap.*

YOUNG TOMMIE 3
Let's set up camp right here.

HUCK
(looking around)
Prob'ly the same place the pirates camped.

JO
(skeptically)
Are you sure there was pirates here?

YOUNG TOMMIE 3
They was here all right, and buried their treasure too. Just ask Huck!

HUCK
Sure, my great-grandpappy helped 'em do the buryin', but he never told nobody where.

JO
And nobody's ever found it in all these years?

YOUNG TOMMIE 3
Nope, but I bet nobody's ever looked as smart as we're goin' to.

JO
What do we do first?

HUCK
First, I'm goin' fishin', so's we don't starve.

> *Huck grabs a fishing pole from
> the prop box and walks away.*

YOUNG TOMMIE 3
Okay, and I'll get the camp set up.

JO
What about me?

YOUNG TOMMIE 3
You got the most important job for findin' the treasure.

JO
Yeah? What?

YOUNG TOMMIE 3
Go all over the island and look for likely diggin' spots. Gosh, there could even be a big "X" on the ground!

JO
Ooh, like on a treasure map?

YOUNG TOMMIE 3
Sure, why not? The pirates needed to find the treasure again somehow.

JO
You want I should look inside the cave?

YOUNG TOMMIE 3
Naw, too scary. Don't go in there alone. Wait till Huck gets back, and we'll all try it.

JO
Oh, okay!

YOUNG TOMMIE 3
You better count how many steps it is around the island.

JO
Okay. One, two, three, four…

> *Jo walks off carefully, counting steps. Young Tommie starts looking through the sacks the runaways brought.*

YOUNG TOMMIE 3
(whistling)
Once there was an island stuffed with gold…

OLD TOMMIE
There I was, lookin' through our supplies, when suddenly I heard laughin' in the distance.

> *Old Tommie points at some Ensemble Members, who burst out laughing. Young Tommie freezes in alarm.*

BECKY'S FAMILY
[laughter]

YOUNG TOMMIE 3
What in tarnation is that?

OLD TOMMIE
It was my bestie Becky Thatcher with her parents and a flock of cousins, just finishin' a picnic on the island.

> *Old Tommie points at Ensemble Members to play BECKY and her family. Becky and COUSIN EMILY (hair bows) enter, then stop when they see Young Tommie.*

BECKY
(surprised but pleased)
Oh!

COUSIN EMILY
(surprised and snooty)
Oh!

YOUNG TOMMIE 3
Oh! Becky! What're you doin' here?

BECKY
We just come over for a family picnic.

COUSIN EMILY
(to Becky, indicating Tommie)
Do you know this... um, person?

BECKY
(to Emily)
This is my best friend, Tommie.
(to Tommie)
This is my Cousin Emily.

YOUNG TOMMIE 3
(to Emily)
Pleased to meetcha, I'm sure.

> *Young Tommie offers a hand, which Emily snootily refuses to touch.*

COUSIN EMILY
(turning away, coldly)
How do you do.

> *Becky's Cousins TRACY and LEE (and any additional cousins) enter laughing.*

TRACY, LEE, OTHER COUSINS
[laughter]

BECKY
What's so funny? Cousin Tracy? Cousin Lee? Anybody?

COUSIN TRACY
We're just laughin' about that picnic...

COUSIN LEE
And how we should call it a pig-nic...

TRACY, LEE, OTHER COUSINS
...Becuz we ate like pigs!

> *The Cousins laugh. BECKY'S FATHER and MOTHER*

enter (bowler hat and parasol).
Becky runs over to them.

BECKY
Mother, Father, look! It's my friend Tommie!

BECKY'S MOTHER
Oh Tommie, Becky has told us so much about you.

BECKY'S FATHER
(to Mother)
She has?

BECKY'S MOTHER
(to Father)
Not really, but be polite and pretend.

BECKY'S FATHER
(to Mother)
Ohhhh!
(to Tommie)
Hello Tommie, we've heard a lot about you.

YOUNG TOMMIE 3
(to Becky)
They have?

BECKY
(to Tommie)
Not really, but be polite and pretend.

YOUNG TOMMIE 3
(to Becky)
Ohhhh!
(to Mother and Father)
Pleased to meetcha, I'm sure.

COUSIN TRACY
(to Tommie)
What're you doin' here, anyway?

COUSIN LEE
We thought this island was deserted.

YOUNG TOMMIE 3
Well it is mostly, only me and my pals are here lookin' for the buried pirate treasure.

COUSIN EMILY
Pshaw! There's no treasure here! You made that up!

YOUNG TOMMIE 3
No, it's true! Why d'ya think they call it Pirate Island?

BECKY'S FAMILY
Pirates! Here?

> *Young Tommie echoes the*
> *interchange Old Tommie had*
> *with the ensemble earlier.*

YOUNG TOMMIE 3
Sure! Ain't you never heard about the Pirates of the Mississippi?

BECKY'S FAMILY
No!

YOUNG TOMMIE 3
Yep, they raided along the river for years, gatherin' loot all the way from Ioway down to New Orleans.

BECKY'S FAMILY
Ooh, really?

YOUNG TOMMIE 3
And they buried their treasure right here on Pirate Island.

BECKY'S FAMILY
Tell us the story!

Music 09: Pirate Island B
Vocal chorus, instrumental interlude, vocal chorus

YOUNG TOMMIE 3, OLD TOMMIE
Once there was an island stuffed with gold,
Hid by pirates raidin' on the river.
Buried all their gold to beat the law,
Ended up in prison down in Arkansas!

> *During the instrumental*
> *interlude, Young Tommie and*
> *Becky's Family yell rhythmically*
> *over the music.*

YOUNG TOMMIE 3
There was gold! (BECKY'S FAMILY: Ooh!)
There was silver! (Ah!)
There was rubies all glowin' and red! (Wow!)
There was pearls! (Ooh!)
There was diamonds! (Ah!)
There was em'ralds as big as your head! (Wow!)

ALL
Once there was an island stuffed with gold,
Hid by pirates raidin' on the river.
Buried all their gold to beat the law,
Ended up in prison down in Arkansas!

TRACY, LEE, OTHER COUSINS
(ad lib)
Ooh, pirate treasure! Maybe we can find it! Just think of all those jewels! C'mon, Emily!

COUSIN EMILY
I refuse to get dirty looking for some imaginary junk.

TRACY, LEE, OTHER COUSINS
(ad lib)
Oh, don't be a spoilsport, Emily! Let's go! Maybe it's over there!

> *The Cousins run off, pulling Emily reluctantly with them.*

BECKY
Mother, can I stay and help Tommie look for the treasure? Can I, Father? Can I, huh?

BECKY'S FATHER
You mean, may I stay.

BECKY'S MOTHER
And no, you may not. Go along with your Cousins.

BECKY
Oh, I'm tired of them.

YOUNG TOMMIE 3
Besides, we don't need your help. Me and Jo and Huck've got it all figured out.

BECKY
Fine! You go on then, and maybe one of them can be your best friend! Becuz it won't be me!

Becky stamps her foot and runs off after the Cousins, trying not to cry.

YOUNG TOMMIE 3
Aw, shucks!

BECKY'S MOTHER
Oh Tommie, now you've hurt her feelings!

BECKY'S FATHER
(sternly)
Young man/lady, that was not very nice.

YOUNG TOMMIE 3
(ashamed)
No it sure wasn't, Mister Thatcher.

BECKY'S MOTHER
(kindly)
Call him Judge, not Mister.

YOUNG TOMMIE 3
I mean Judge Thatcher.

BECKY'S FATHER
Never mind that now.
(to Becky's Mother)
We'd better go find her.

BECKY'S MOTHER
(to Becky's Father)
Good idea.
(calling off)
Becky! Becky!

BECKY'S FATHER
(calling off)
Becky!

Becky's Father and Mother exit after Becky.

OLD TOMMIE
I felt kinda bad about Becky, but darn it, why'd she have to get all upset becuz I told her the truth?

YOUNG TOMMIE 3
(muttering and kicking the dirt)
Aw, shucks.

The Cousins run on. They are crying and yelling over each other.

TRACY, LEE, EMILY, COUSINS
Help! Help!

COUSIN TRACY
Becky went in the cave!

COUSIN LEE
We couldn't stop her!

COUSIN EMILY
And it's all your fault!

TRACY, LEE, EMILY, COUSINS
Help! Help!

YOUNG TOMMIE 3
Huh? What? Slow down and tell me what happened.

COUSIN TRACY
Becky came running up, all crying and upset…

COUSIN LEE
She said she would find the treasure all by herself…

COUSIN EMILY
Just to show you how wrong you were!

TRACY, LEE, EMILY, COUSINS
She's lost in the cave!

Young Tommie becomes very decisive. During the following lines, he/she unpacks a lantern and "lights" it.

NOTE: *The lantern needs to be lit and unlit at different times. You can either use a battery-run light that can be manually switched on/off or just pretend the lantern goes on/off.*

YOUNG TOMMIE 3
Did she have a map of the cave?

COUSIN TRACY
No.

YOUNG TOMMIE 3
Did she have a shovel?

COUSIN LEE
No.

YOUNG TOMMIE 3
Did she have a lantern?

COUSIN EMILY
No.

YOUNG TOMMIE 3
Well, I don't have a map, but I'll take a shovel and lantern in to find her.

> *Young Tommie takes the lantern and a shovel and starts off. One by one, the Cousins get in the way.*

COUSIN TRACY
(standing in Tommie's way)
You're going in?

YOUNG TOMMIE 3
(trying to get around)
Yep.

COUSIN LEE
(standing in Tommie's way)
All by yourself?

YOUNG TOMMIE 3
(trying to get around)
Yep.

COUSIN EMILY
(standing in Tommie's way)
You ought to. After all, it's your fault she went in there.

YOUNG TOMMIE 3
(trying to get around)
Yep.

TRACY, LEE, EMILY, COUSINS
(ad lib)
Yep?!? You agree with Emily? You think it's all your fault?

YOUNG TOMMIE 3
(finally getting around the cousins)
Yep! Now leave me be!

> *Young Tommie walks in place as though moving toward the cave. The Cousins fade back or sit down.*

OLD TOMMIE
So off I went. I was honor-bound to save my bestie Becky.

> *Old Tommie points to two Ensemble Members to form the cave entrance.*

OLD TOMMIE
(continued)
When I got to the cave entrance, I paused a sec to rustle up all my nerve.

YOUNG TOMMIE 3
Okay, I gotta go in. Just think how lonesome and scared Becky must be!

> *Young Tommie holds up the lantern and passes through the cave entrance. The Ensemble Members fade back.*

OLD TOMMIE
Yep, that cave was mighty dark and mighty scary, but the worst part was still to come.

YOUNG TOMMIE 3
Becky!

> *Old Tommie points to Ensemble Members to be the "echoes."*

ECHOES
(fading gradually)
Becky! Becky! Becky! Becky! Becky!

YOUNG TOMMIE 3
(startled)
What's that? Oh, it's only an *(calling out)* echo.

ECHOES
(fading gradually)
Echo! Echo! Echo! Echo! Echo!

YOUNG TOMMIE 3
Whew! As long as it ain't ghosts, I'm okay.

OLD TOMMIE
No sooner did I think about ghosts, when I started to hear 'em whistlin' through the cave.

> *Old Tommie points to Ensemble Members to be the whistling wind.*

WHISTLING WIND
(spookily)
Ooooooooooooooooh! Ooooooooh!

> *Young Tommie almost drops the lantern.*

YOUNG TOMMIE 3
Oh! Ghosts! I better get outta here!

> *Young Tommie starts to leave, then stops and turns as Old Tommie describes.*

OLD TOMMIE
I was darned scared, but then I thought of how much worse Becky must feel, and I determined to keep goin'.

YOUNG TOMMIE 3
(to him/herself)
It's only the wind. It's only the wind.
(calling)
Becky!

ECHOES
(fading gradually)
Becky! Becky! Becky! Becky! Becky!

OLD TOMMIE
Just then I heard a new noise, like somebody crying.

BECKY
(crying)
Oh Tommie, where are you? I'm all alone!

ECHOES
(fading gradually)
Lone! Lone! Lone! Lone! Lone!

> *Becky sits, curled up and sobbing, as if against a cave wall.*

NOTE: Have Ensemble Members hold up a faintly X-marked wall if desired.

YOUNG TOMMIE 3
Here I come, Becky!

ECHOES
(fading gradually)
Becky! Becky! Becky! Becky! Becky!

> *Tommie stands in front of Becky, holding up the lantern.*

YOUNG TOMMIE 3
Becky! Are you okay?

BECKY
Oh Tommie, you found me! I was so scared!

OLD TOMMIE
Suddenly, the light shone on the wall behind Becky's head.

YOUNG TOMMIE 3
(gasping)
Jumpin' jeepers, look at that!

BECKY
(turning to look)
What? What is it?

YOUNG TOMMIE 3
(pointing)
There's a big X on the wall!

BECKY
(turning to look)
There is?

YOUNG TOMMIE 3
You found the treasure!

BECKY
I did?

YOUNG TOMMIE 3
All these years, people been looking at the ground…

BECKY
…and it was buried in the cave wall all the time!

YOUNG TOMMIE 3, BECKY
(dancing and jumping with joy)
We found it! We found it!
(stopping in alarm)
What's that?

OLD TOMMIE
Suddenly I could hear them ghosts again.

WHISTLING WIND
(spookily)
Oooooooooooooooh! Oooooooooh!

Young Tommie drops the lantern, which goes out. Becky and Young Tommie cling together and stare blankly around as though they can't see.

BECKY
Oh! Now it's all dark! What're we gonna do?

YOUNG TOMMIE 3
I reckon all we can do is hold tight and call for help.

YOUNG TOMMIE 3, BECKY
(calling)
Help! Help!

ECHOES
(fading gradually)
Help! Help! Help! Help! Help!

OLD TOMMIE
Through all the echoing racket, I thought I could hear somethin' else.

> *Huck lights the other lantern from the Prop Box and holds/mimes a fishing line, giving the other end to Becky's Father. Young Tommie shushes Becky and listens blindly through the echoes.*

NOTE: An imaginary fishing line works just as well as a real one, as long as the actors mime it consistently.

YOUNG TOMMIE 3
Ssh! Did you hear that?

HUCK
(in the distance)
Tommie! Tommie!

ECHOES
(fading gradually)
Tommie! Tommie! Tommie! Tommie! Tommie!

YOUNG TOMMIE 3
Cheer up, Becky, we're saved!
(calling)
Here we are, Huck!

ECHOES
(fading gradually)
Huck! Huck! Huck! Huck! Huck!

HUCK
(getting closer)
Tommie! Tommie!

YOUNG TOMMIE 3, BECKY
(calling)
Huck! Huck!

ECHOES
(overlapping)
Tommie! Huck! Tommie! Huck! Tommie! Huck!

> *The calling and echoing continue*
> *until Huck reaches Young*
> *Tommie and Becky.*

HUCK
(holding up his lantern)
There y'all are!

YOUNG TOMMIE 3
Huck, am I glad to see you!

BECKY
Me too!

HUCK
Well, come on! I brung a fishin' line, and it leads right back to your Pappy, Becky.

BECKY
Back to Father! Let's hurry!

YOUNG TOMMIE 3
Wait! We need to mark this spot so's we can find it again.

HUCK
Why?

YOUNG TOMMIE 3
(pointing at the X)
Looky there, Huck! It's the treasure!

HUCK
(holding up the lantern)
Well gosh—it sure is!

YOUNG TOMMIE 3
Let's tie that line to my shovel and leave it here.

HUCK, BECKY
Good idea!

They tie the line to the shovel, then start following the other end out.

HUCK, BECKY, YOUNG TOMMIE 3
(calling)
Here we come! We're safe!

ECHOES
(fading gradually)
Safe! Safe! Safe! Safe! Safe!

The calling and echoing continue until they pass through the cave entrance (same Ensemble Members as before). Becky's Family are waiting for them, with her father holding the end of the line.

BECKY
(rushing to them)
Mother! Father! Cousins!

BECKY'S FAMILY
(ad lib)
Hurray! Becky! Thank goodness, you're safe!

OLD TOMMIE
All the Thatchers started huggin' and cryin'. Me and Huck tried to sneak away becuz we were so embarrassed.

YOUNG TOMMIE 3
C'mon, Huck!

HUCK
Yep, let's get outta here.

BECKY
Wait, Tommie! Tell my folks about the treasure!

BECKY'S FAMILY
(ad lib)
The treasure! What about it?

BECKY
We found it in the cave!

YOUNG TOMMIE 3
Well, Becky did.

COUSIN TRACY
What a whiz!

COUSIN LEE
What a thrill!

COUSIN EMILY
What a bunch of lies!

TRACY, LEE, COUSINS
(to Emily, ad lib)
Ssh! Don't be such a spoilsport! Oh Emily! Do hush up!

YOUNG TOMMIE 3
We found a great big X. Didn't we, Huck?

HUCK
Yep, and it's right at the end of this line.

BECKY'S FAMILY
Hurray!

BECKY'S FATHER
Then we can come back later and dig for the treasure!

BECKY'S MOTHER
And split it between Tommie and Becky and this boy...

YOUNG TOMMIE 3
Huck!

HUCK
What about Jo?

YOUNG TOMMIE 3
Oh yeah—what about Jo?

Jo enters, looking down and still counting steps. He/she is surprised to find a crowd.

JO
...four thousand nine hundred and two, four thousand nine hundred... Oh!

YOUNG TOMMIE 3
Hey Jo! Guess what we did while you were gone?

JO
What?

YOUNG TOMMIE 3
Found the treasure, that's all.

JO
What!?!

YOUNG TOMMIE 3
But don't worry—we'll split it with you!

HUCK, BECKY
Sure, we'll split it with you!

OLD TOMMIE
And that's how I—with a little help—

ALL
—found the treasure!

Young Tommie, Becky and Huck join hands and dance around Jo, who seems confused. Becky's Family join hands in a large circle.

Music 10: Pirate Island C
Vocal chorus, instrumental interlude, vocal chorus

TOMMIES, BECKY, HUCK
Once there was an island stuffed with gold,
Hid by pirates raidin' on the river.
Buried all their gold to beat the law,
Ended up in prison down in Arkansas!

> *During the instrumental interlude, Young Tommie, Becky, Jo and Huck yell rhythmically over the music, with Becky's Family responding. Old Tommie chuckles quietly.*

YOUNG TOMMIE 3, BECKY, JO, HUCK
We got gold! (BECKY'S FAMILY: Ooh!)
We got silver! (Ah!)
We got rubies all glowin' and red! (Wow!)
We got pearls! (Ooh!)
We got diamonds! (Ah!)
We got em'ralds as big as your head! (Wow!)

ALL
Once there was an island stuffed with gold,
Hid by pirates raidin' on the river.
Buried all their gold to beat the law,
Ended up in prison down in Arkansas!

> CONTINUE WITH THE CLOSING

Closing: Old Tommie's Stories

> *The Ensemble Members are seated around Old Tommie, the same as in the Opening.*

OLD TOMMIE
So that's the way it was when I was a young'un.

ENSEMBLE 6
(sincerely)
Tommie, are your stories true or did you make them up?

OLD TOMMIE
They all really happened.

A FEW ENSEMBLE MEMBERS
Really?

OLD TOMMIE
Well, I added a little trimmin'…

ENSEMBLE MEMBERS
(disappointed)
Oh!

OLD TOMMIE
But only a little!

ENSEMBLE MEMBERS
(happily)
Oh!

ENSEMBLE 7
Can we come back tomorrow?

OLD TOMMIE
Sure! I got lots more to tell you!

ENSEMBLE MEMBERS
Yay! Old Tommie!

> *The ensemble sings and marches around Old Tommie.*

Music 11: When Tommie Tells Stories B
Vocal chorus, instrumental chorus, vocal chorus

ALL
When Tommie tells stories, we all cheer
Hurrah! Hurrah!
Old Tommie has tales we love to hear
Hurrah! Hurrah!
At first we'll cheer, and then we'll shout,
As Tommie brings all the mischief out.
And we'll sing and play
When Tommie starts telling tales!

During the instrumental, the
Young Tommies lead a cheer.

YOUNG TOMMIE 1
(over the music)
Three cheers for Old Tommie! Hip hip—

ENSEMBLE MEMBERS
Hurray!

YOUNG TOMMIES
Hip hip—

ENSEMBLE MEMBERS
Hurray!

YOUNG TOMMIES
Hip hip—

ENSEMBLE MEMBERS
Hurray!

ALL
When Tommie tells stories, we all cheer
Hurrah! Hurrah!
Old Tommie has tales we love to hear
Hurrah! Hurrah!
At first we'll cheer, and then we'll shout,
As Tommie brings all the mischief out.
And we'll sing and play
When Tommie starts telling tales!

THE END

ALADDIN AND THE MAGIC LAMP

CHARACTERS

Aladdin	M	Poor bazaar boy, pickpocket but goodhearted
Princess Armina	F	Feisty princess, sometimes shy but often bold
Genie	M or F	Wisecracking supernatural being
Sultan	M	Bored king
Sultaness	F	Bored queen
Vizier	M	Evil villain, prime minister
Mother	F	Aladdin's mother, doing her best to get by
Landlord/lady	M or F	Stern owner of Mother's bazaar cart
Snake Tamer/ Snake	M or F	Plays both the snake and the tamer; snake is a puppet
Burly	M or F	Palace Guards
Surly	M or F	
Curly	M or F	
Layla	F	Princess Armina's friends
Zayla	F	
Kayla	F	
Magick	M or F	Genie's assistants; double as ensemble in the first number
Mysterie	M or F	

3 M, 6 F, 8 M or F, plus ensemble

Many roles can be doubled or combined

SET

Somewhere in Persia, or maybe Araby

    Scene 1: Marketplace (Songs: *In a Persian Market, The Rent Song*)

    Scene 2: Cave (inside & outside) (Song: *Rings on My Fingers*)

    Scene 3: Marketplace (Song: *Rings on My Fingers*)

    Scene 4: Palace (Song: *The Sheik of Araby*)

    Scene 5: Marketplace (Songs: *New Lamps for Old, Rings on My Fingers*)

LENGTH

30 minutes

Scene 1: Marketplace

A few carts with merchandise for sale (fruit, spices, etc.).

The ENSEMBLE is onstage. They sing in three groups: SELLERS (including MOTHER), BUYERS (including the LANDLORD/LADY) and ENTERTAINERS (including the SNAKE TAMER and a few jugglers). Some Buyers pause to watch the entertainment. ALADDIN mingles, stealing food and picking pockets.

Music 01: In a Persian Market A
Tune: In a Persian Market (tone poem by Ketelbey, 1920)
Instrumental interlude, Vocal chorus, Instrumental interlude, Vocal chorus

---

SELLERS
Lemons, perfume, spices to buy!

BUYERS
Not for me, your price is too high!

ENTERTAINERS
See our tricks, and watch the time fly!

ALL
In a Persian Market!

SELLERS
(ad lib, at the same time)
Lemons! Fresh ripe Lemons!
Perfumes from distant lands!
Spices! Cinnamon, ginger, cloves!

BUYERS
(ad lib, at the same time)
I'll take two of those.
I won't pay more than three for that!
Quick now, I want to get home for supper.

ENTERTAINERS
(ad lib, at the same time)
We perform the finest tricks!
Watch closely and you'll be amazed!
We're the world's greatest entertainers!

SELLERS
Lemons, perfume, spices to buy!

BUYERS
Not for me, your price is too high!

ENTERTAINERS
See our tricks, and watch the time fly!

ALL
In a Persian Market!

> *The Guards (BURLY, SURLY and CURLY) enter, carrying spears.*

BURLY
Make way for the magnificent Sultan!

> *The crowd cheers half-heartedly.*

SURLY
And the glorious Sultaness!

> *The crowd cheers half-heartedly.*

CURLY
Make way for the radiant Princess Armina!

> *The crowd cheers enthusiastically. The VIZIER enters.*

VIZIER
Excuse me guard, aren't you forgetting someone?

BURLY
Oh yes, and the mighty Vizier is coming too.

> *The crowd groans.*

VIZIER
Ah, I see that I am as popular as ever.
(to the Snake Tamer)
You there!

> *The Snake Tamer approaches nervously.*

Note: Use the old-fashioned trick of a snake puppet in a basket that is attached to the Tamer with a fake arm. The same actor performs both the Snake and the Snake Tamer.

SNAKE TAMER
Yes, O great one? You wish to talk with my humble self?

SNAKE
Yesss, sssilly, that's why he called usss.

SNAKE TAMER
Ssh!

VIZIER
Is that snake really tame?

SNAKE TAMER
Oh yes, great one. Watch this dance.

SFX: Snake Dance

SNAKE
(Dancing and hissing)
Sss-sss-sss-sss.

> *While the snake is dancing, Aladdin sneaks up behind the Vizier and picks a coin from his pocket.*

VIZIER
Good, you can come work for me.

SNAKE TAMER
O great one! I am not worthy of this honor.

SNAKE
You may not be worthy, but I am! Let'sss go!

> *From now on, the Snake Tamer follows the Vizier everywhere.*

SURLY
The Sultan and the Sultaness approach!

CURLY
Bow everyone! The Princess approaches!

SFX: Fanfare

> *The guards stand at attention. The SULTAN and SULTANESS enter, waving to the crowd. The PRINCESS follows them, a little shy. Her friends (LAYLA, ZAYLA and KAYLA) follow, waving fans or flags. The crowd cheers; the Vizier watches.*

SULTAN
Greetings, all you lowly townsfolk!

SULTANESS
We are here to give you the pleasure of looking at us!

SULTAN
We know you get so little pleasure in your humdrum lives.

SULTANESS
Isn't it kind of us to come all the way out here?

> *The crowd cheers half-heartedly. Everyone looks at the Princess.*

LAYLA
Do speak up, Princess, everyone is waiting.

ZAYLA
It's your duty to greet the crowds.

KAYLA
Go ahead, Princess, don't be shy.

PRINCESS
Hello there…

The Princess is paralyzed with shyness.

LANDLORD
We can't hear you! Speak up already!

MOTHER
Be nice to the poor girl!

ALADDIN
She's so beautiful!

The Princess opens her mouth but nothing comes out. The crowd turns away in disgust.

SULTAN
Well, I guess we'll be heading back to the palace.

SULTANESS
This procession was a waste of time!

VIZIER
Guards! Back to the palace!

SFX: Fanfare

The Guards, Sultan & Sultaness, and Friends exit, followed by the Vizier and Snake Tamer. The jugglers start their act again. The Princess ducks down and stays to watch. She laughs and claps in delight.

PRINCESS
Bravo! Wonderful!

Aladdin moves closer, intending to pick her pocket.

ALADDIN
Wait! Aren't you the Princess?

PRINCESS
Shh! No one knows I'm here!

ALADDIN
(whispering)
I can keep a secret.

PRINCESS
(whispering)
I just needed to get away.

ALADDIN
You don't seem so shy any more.

PRINCESS
I'm not really shy, only in front of a crowd.

The Friends rush back in.

LAYLA
There you are, Princess!

ZAYLA
Princess, we were so worried about you!

KAYLA
Come with us now!

PRINCESS
All right.
(suddenly shy again, to Aladdin)
Goodbye.

ALADDIN
Goodbye.

The Princess and Friends exit.

ALADDIN
Wow! I can't believe a Princess was talking to a poor boy like me! I'll watch her as long as I can.

Aladdin exits. The crowd starts to disperse, singing as they go.

Music 02: In a Persian Market B
Vocal chorus with ending

SELLERS
Lemons, perfume, spices to buy!

BUYERS
Not for me, your price is too high!

ENTERTAINERS
See our tricks, and watch the time fly!

ALL
In a Persian Market!

> *The market is empty, except for Mother at her cart.*

MOTHER
(singing to herself)
In a Persian Market!
(looking around)
Where is my son Aladdin? He should be here by now.

> *The Landlord/lady enters.*

LANDLORD
I need to talk with you.

MOTHER
Oh no!

LANDLORD
It's time to pay the rent on this cart, or I'll take it back.

MOTHER
Please give me just one more day!

LANDLORD
You must pay the rent!

MOTHER
I can't pay the rent!

> *The Landlord and Mother burst into a showy, overly-operatic song. When Aladdin arrives, he joins in in the same melodramatic style.*

> **Music 03: The Rent Song**
> **Tune: Vesti la giubba ("No more Rice Krispies!") (from "Pagliacci" by Leoncavallo, 1892)**
> **Two vocal choruses**

LANDLORD
Must pay the rent!
Yes, you must pay the rent!

MOTHER
Can't pay the rent!
Oh no I can't pay the rent!

> *Aladdin enters.*

ALADDIN
I'll pay the rent!
Oh yes I'll pay the rent!

LANDLORD MOTHER
He'll pay the rent!

ALL THREE
Oh yes he (I) will pay the rent!

> *Aladdin gives the Landlord the coin he stole from the Vizier.*

MOTHER
My son, the hero!

LANDLORD
Curses!

ALADDIN
You have your money, now go!

> *Landlord crosses away from the cart and stands examining the coin.*

MOTHER
Aladdin, where did you get the money?

ALADDIN
Never mind. Go home, I'll watch the cart.

MOTHER
Oh Aladdin, I worry about you sometimes.

ALADDIN
It's all right, Mother. Now come along.

Aladdin escorts Mother off in one direction, while the Vizier and Snake Tamer enter from the other. They are looking on the ground.

VIZIER
It's a rare old coin. I must have it back!

SNAKE
Let me down, and I'll sssearch for it.

SNAKE TAMER
No, you'd slither away and I'd never see you again.

SNAKE
That'sss the idea!

The Vizier sees the Landlord holding the coin.

VIZIER
Hey! Where did you get that? Give it to me!

LANDLORD
It's mine. I got it from the boy in there, to pay the rent.

VIZIER
Well, you'll give it to me, or get bitten by this snake!

SNAKE
Oh pleassse. I'm not hungry right now.

SNAKE TAMER
Bite! Bite! Bite!

The Snake hisses and threatens to bite the Landlord.

LANDLORD
Aaaaah! Take it! Take it!

The Landlord throws down the coin and runs offstage. The Vizier picks it up just as Aladdin reenters.

VIZIER
You, boy! How did you get this coin?

ALADDIN
Oh, ah, well, I um—

VIZIER
You stole it, didn't you?

ALADDIN
Well, we needed to pay the rent, and my mother was hungry...

VIZIER
Do I look like I care? Hmm, I think I can use you to run an errand for me.

ALADDIN
I need to stay here and mind the store!

VIZIER
You can run my errand, or I can call the guards and you can rot in jail. Which do you prefer?

ALADDIN
(pointing to the Tamer)
Why can't he/she go?

VIZIER
It's a dangerous job.

SNAKE TAMER
Awww! You like me!

VIZIER
No, I like the snake.

SNAKE
Sssee, I told you I wasss lovable!

VIZIER
(to Aladdin)
Well?

ALADDIN
All right. What do I have to do?

VIZIER
Walk this way…

The Vizier exits, followed by Aladdin imitating his walk.

SNAKE TAMER
Ooh, I wonder what is so dangerous?

SNAKE
Ssso walk that way, and we'll sssee.

The Snake Tamer follows them off with the same walk.

END OF SCENE 1

Scene 2: Cave (inside & outside)

The Vizier, Aladdin and Snake Tamer/Snake enter in front of the curtain. The curtain is open a little to make the cave entrance.

ALADDIN
Can we stop a minute? I'm exhausted!

SNAKE TAMER
I have a ton of sand in my shoes!

SNAKE
There'sss even sssand in my basssket!

VIZIER
Oh, quit your complaining. We're here.

Aladdin and Snake Tamer/Snake look around.

SNAKE TAMER
We're here?

SNAKE
Where'sss thisss?

ALADDIN
What are we doing out here?

VIZIER
There's something I need inside this cave. You, boy, go in and get it.

ALADDIN
That's all I have to do?

VIZIER
Yes, you'll find an antique lamp in there. Get it for me.

ALADDIN
We came all the way out here for an old lamp?

VIZIER
Yes, it has sentimental value.

SNAKE TAMER
Sentimental value?

SNAKE
I didn't realize the Vizier had any sssentimentsss.

ALADDIN
All right then, here I go.

Aladdin goes through the curtain into the cave.

SNAKE TAMER
Why don't you just get it yourself?

VIZIER
There's danger of a cave-in. Besides, I'm scared of *(he shudders)* bats.

SNAKE
Batsss! Tasssty!

SFX: Rumbling

Sudden rumbling. The Vizier and Snake Tamer/Snake shake like there's an earthquake. The curtains start to close.

SNAKE TAMER
Oh no!

SNAKE
Oh no!

VIZIER
Oh no!

Aladdin sticks his head out through the curtain.

ALADDIN
Help!

The curtains close completely and Aladdin's head disappears.

SNAKE TAMER
Oh how terrible!

SNAKE
Oh how sssad!

VIZIER
Oh how irritating. Let's go back to town.

The Vizier and Snake Tamer/Snake exit back to town

SNAKE TAMER
(as they exit)
I wonder how's he doing in there.

SNAKE
Me alssso!

The curtains open as they exit, revealing the interior of the cave. Aladdin is lying on the floor. There are a few rocks, one with the lamp on it. Aladdin stands up.

ALADDIN
Now I'm trapped! At least there's a little light. But I can't see if there's a way out.

He peers around and sees the lamp.

ALADDIN
Maybe that lamp still works.

He picks up the lamp and examines it. He tries to rub some dirt off of it. Suddenly the lamp comes to life and starts pulling him in different directions.

SFX: Lamp Magic (Long)

ALADDIN
Whoa! Hey! Stop that!

ALADDIN AND THE MAGIC LAMP

> *The lamp pulls him to the edge of the stage. When Aladdin pulls the lamp back on, the GENIE is holding the other end.*

GENIE
Woohoo! I'm outta there! Now I can dance!

> *The Genie dances around the stage.*

SFX: Genie Dance

GENIE
And I can breathe the fresh air! *(takes a deep breath and chokes)* Ooh, where am I? It's like being back in the lamp again.

ALADDIN
Who are you?

GENIE
(startled)
Oh, there you are! Well, master, tell me your wishes.

ALADDIN
What?

GENIE
(explaining slowly)
I am a Genie. You rubbed the lamp. You get three wishes.

ALADDIN
I get three wishes?

GENIE
I just said that. Geez! Don't kids read fairy tales anymore?

ALADDIN
Three wishes! Well, the first one is obvious. I wish to be out of this cave!

GENIE
All right! A little lamp magic music, please!

> *The Genie claps his/her hands.*

SFX: Lamp Magic (Long)

The Genie and Aladdin twirl around and end up in front of the closed curtain. Aladdin is still holding the lamp.

ALADDIN
Wow! That was some magic!

GENIE
Thank you, thank you. It's good to know I haven't lost my touch. Now what comes next?

ALADDIN
Hmm, what else do I wish? Any ideas?

GENIE
(rubbing fingers together to indicate money)
Duh. It's usually the first thing people wish for.

ALADDIN
Oh yeah! Money! I wish to be rich—wait, not just rich, a rich prince!

GENIE
Ooh, now *that's* original. Here we go!

The Genie claps his/her hands.

SFX: Lamp Magic

MAGICK and MYSTERIE, the Genie's assistants enter, with a chest of jewels and gold, plus a fancy turban and cape for Aladdin.

GENIE
This is my favorite part!

Music 04: Rings on Your Fingers A
Tune: I've Got Rings on My Fingers (Weston and Barnes, 1909)
Vocal chorus, instrumental interlude, Vocal chorus

GENIE
Now you've got...
Rings on your fingers,
Bells on your toes,

ALADDIN AND THE MAGIC LAMP

An elephant trunk pokes through the curtains.

GENIE
Elephants to ride upon,
And diamonds, goodness knows!
A turban with jewels,
A cape with gold inlay,
You're the Prince of Mumbo-Jumbo
Jijiboo Jay. OK!

More music while the assistants finish dressing Aladdin.

ALADDIN
(over the music)
Wow! Look at me!

GENIE
Looking good!

ALADDIN
Let's go show my Mother!

ALADDIN
Now I've got…
Rings on my fingers,
Bells on my toes,
Elephants to ride upon,
And diamonds, goodness knows!

ALADDIN, GENIE, ASSISTANTS
A turban with jewels,
A cape with gold inlay,
I'm (You're) the Prince of Mumbo-Jumbo
Jijiboo Jay. OK!

Aladdin and the Genie exit, followed by the Assistants. The curtain opens.

END OF SCENE 2

Scene 3: Marketplace

Ensemble is selling and buying. Aladdin's mother is busy at her cart. The Landlord/lady is shopping.

MOTHER
(looking around)
I wonder what happened to Aladdin?

LANDLORD
He'd better come back, or you'll lose this cart and all your miserable merchandise.

MOTHER
Aladdin is a good boy. He'll come home.

The crowd begins to murmur, looking offstage to where Aladdin and the Genie will enter.

LANDLORD
I wonder what is happening over there?

MOTHER
Whatever it is, it's coming this way.

Music 05: Rings on Your Fingers B
Vocal chorus

Aladdin and the Genie enter, followed by the Assistants. All are singing.

ALADDIN, GENIE, ASSISTANTS
Now I've (he's) got…
Rings on my (his) fingers,
Bells on my (his) toes,
Elephants to ride upon,
And diamonds, goodness knows!
A turban with jewels,
A cape with gold inlay,
I'm (He's) the Prince of Mumbo-Jumbo
Jijiboo Jay. OK!

ENSEMBLE
(ad lib, as the music ends)
A Prince! Look at that turban! He looks so grand! I've never seen him before!

Aladdin throws some coins to the crowd. They (including the Landlord) scramble to pick them up. Aladdin directs the assistants to keep throwing coins, then crosses to the cart, followed by the Genie.

MOTHER
Your highness, I am so honored!

ALADDIN
Mother, don't you recognize me?

MOTHER
Aladdin! Where did you get those clothes?

GENIE
Don't tell her.

ALADDIN
It's a long story. I've come to take you to the palace!

MOTHER
Oh no, I'd rather stay here.

GENIE
Mothers! They're all a little crazy.

ALADDIN
Hey, don't talk about my mother that way.

MOTHER
Who are you talking to?

GENIE
She can't see me or hear me.

ALADDIN
Oh. Well, Mother, I'm going up to the palace—

GENIE
Oh, don't tell me—there's a beautiful princess involved! I should have known!

MOTHER
Be careful up there, Aladdin.

ALADDIN
Yes, Mother. Here's some gold. Buy yourself something nice.

Aladdin gives Mother some coins.

MOTHER
Oh my goodness!

ALADDIN
Oh, and Mother, will you watch this for me?

Aladdin gives her the lamp. The crowd has finished picking up the coins and gathers around Aladdin, pulling him away from the cart.

MOTHER
Now, why does he want this old lamp?

Mother puts the lamp on a shelf in the cart.

GENIE
(calling after Aladdin)
Wait, now I have to stay here with the lamp. And I can't go back inside until you make your third wish! Wait!
(giving up)
Oh that's fine. Just fine.

The Genie and assistants stay by the cart while the curtains close. The crowd and Aladdin sing.

Music 06: Rings on Your Fingers C
Vocal chorus

ALADDIN, ENSEMBLE
Now I've (he's) got…
Rings on my (his) fingers,
Bells on my (his) toes,
Elephants to ride upon,

And diamonds, goodness knows!
A turban with jewels,
A cape with gold inlay,
I'm (He's) the Prince of Mumbo-Jumbo
Jijiboo Jay. OK!

At the end of the song, Aladdin exits toward the palace. The crowd waves goodbye.

END OF SCENE 3

Scene 4: Palace

The Sultan and Sultaness are sitting on their thrones. The Guards are standing nearby.

SULTANESS
(sighing)
I'm bored. Is there anything to do?

SULTAN
Well, we took our stroll among the people...

SULTANESS
I'm sure that was exciting for them, but it wasn't for me!

SULTAN
We could play parcheesi, I suppose.

SULTANESS
I miss the old days, when you were a dashing young sheik.

SULTAN
Oh, I remember! I used to sing to you like this...

Music 07: The Sheik of Araby A
Tune: The Sheik of Araby (Smith, Wheeler & Snyder, 1921)
Vocal chorus

SULTAN
I'm the Sheik of Araby,
Your heart belongs to me!

SULTANESS
At night, when I'm asleep,
Into my dreams you'll creep.

The Guards decide to join in. The Sultan and Sultaness dance and "scat".

SULTAN, SULTANESS, GUARDS
The stars that shine above, (S+S: Oh, how they shine!)
Will light our way to love! (S+S: So much in love!)
You'll rule this land with me, (S+S: Oh yes I will!)
The Sheik of Araby.

SULTAN
(over the ending music)
I'm the Sheik!

SULTANESS
Now <u>that</u> was fun!

SULTAN
I feel like a boy again!

> *The Princess enters; her Friends follow.*

PRINCESS
Papa, Mama, may I speak to you?

SULTANESS
Of course, dear.

> *The Guards lean in to listen*

PRINCESS
I mean, without the Guards listening in?

SULTAN
(to the Guards)
You may go.

> *The Guards exit in disappointment.*

GUARDS
(ad lib, as they exit)
Oh fine! We never get to have any fun! It's not fair!

PRINCESS
When we were in the market today—

LAYLA
She hid from us!

ZAYLA
It's not our fault!

KAYLA
She was so sneaky!

The Princess glares at her friends.

PRINCESS
Do you mind? Anyway, I met this young man—

SULTANESS
Oh no!

SULTAN
Don't say you fell in love with him!

LAYLA
She certainly did!

ZAYLA
She's been blushing all day!

KAYLA
And sighing like this.

The Friends all sigh dramatically.

FRIENDS
Aaah!

PRINCESS
Well—

SFX: Fanfare

The Guards run in.

BURLY
A man just rode up on an elephant!

SURLY
He's covered in jewels!

CURLY
He says he's the Prince of Mumbo-Jumbo!

SULTANESS
Mumbo-Jumbo? Where is that?

ALADDIN AND THE MAGIC LAMP

SULTAN
(to the Guards)
Well, show him in!

> *The Guards exit.*

PRINCESS
But I'm trying to tell you something important!

SULTANESS
Not now, this sounds much more exciting!

SULTAN
It's better than playing parcheesi!

> *Aladdin enters, carrying a chest of jewels.*

SULTAN, SULTANESS
Welcome!

ALADDIN
I bring you greetings from a far land, and as a token of my esteem, a few jewels.

> *He opens the chest of jewels. All gasp.*

SULTANESS
Oh my!

SULTAN
There's a fortune here!

> *The Sultan and Sultaness spend the rest of the scene running their hands through the jewels in fascination.*

ALADDIN
Princess, I have heard so much of your beauty, but now that I see you in person—

PRINCESS
Oh, never mind the flattery.

ALADDIN
(drawing her aside)
You aren't as shy as you were this morning.

PRINCESS
This morning? *(looking at him)* It's you!

ALADDIN
Yes, Princess. I had to see you again.

PRINCESS
Who are you, really?

ALADDIN
Nobody. But I know who I'd like to be.

Music 08: Sheik of Araby B
Vocal verse and chorus

ALADDIN
Over the desert wild and free,
Rides the bold Sheik of Araby.

PRINCESS
His love waits there, under the palms,
He sings to call her to his arms!

ALADDIN
I'm the Sheik of Araby,
Your heart belongs to me!

PRINCESS
At night, when I'm asleep, (FRIENDS: Ooh!)
Into my dreams you'll creep. (FRIENDS: Ooh!)

ALADDIN, PRINCESS
The stars that shine above, (FRIENDS: Oh, how they shine!)
Will light our way to love! (FRIENDS: So much in love!)

ALADDIN
You'll rule this land with me, (FRIENDS: Oh yes she will!)

ALADDIN, PRINCESS, FRIENDS
The Sheik of Araby.

Aladdin and the Princess end the song gazing into each other's eyes. The Vizier enters, the Snake Tamer/Snake following.

ALADDIN AND THE MAGIC LAMP

SULTANESS
Oh there you are, Vizier! Look at these wonderful jewels!

SULTAN
And the nice young Prince who brought them.

VIZIER
(bowing to Aladdin)
Your highness. I always like to meet Princes who bring gifts.

ALADDIN
(mumbling and avoiding the Vizier's eyes)
Your excellency.

PRINCESS
Prince, come see the garden.

Aladdin and the Princess exit. The Vizier watches them leave, then pulls the Snake Tamer/Snake downstage. The curtains close.

VIZIER
Does that Prince look familiar to you?

SNAKE TAMER
Uh, no. *(to the snake)* What about you?

SNAKE
He looksss sssussspisssiousss.

VIZIER
(suddenly realizing)
Aha! It's that brat from the market. He must have survived the cave-in and found the lamp.

SNAKE TAMER
Oh!

SNAKE
Yesss.

VIZIER
Hmm, he doesn't have the lamp with him. Maybe he left it with his mother. Aha! Come with me, I have an evil plan!

SNAKE TAMER
I love evil plans.

SNAKE
Isss there any other kind?

The Vizier exits with the Snake Tamer/Snake. The curtains open.

END OF SCENE 4

Scene 5: Marketplace

The Genie is sitting by Mother's cart, looking into a mirror.

GENIE
(singing a capella)
**I'm the Sheik of Araby,
My heart belongs to me...**

Mother enters, wearing a gaudy new costume piece.

MOTHER
I can't wait to show Aladdin what I've bought!

GENIE
I don't like it, and I don't think he will either.

MOTHER
He'll be so impressed!

GENIE
Why do I bother? She can't hear me.

The Vizier enters. The Snake Tamer/Snake follows, carrying a basket with new lamps.

**Music 09: New Lamps for Old
Two vocal choruses**

VIZIER, SNAKE TAMER
**New Lamps for Old!
Trading New Lamps for Old!**

MOTHER
**New Lamps for Old?
I could trade in this old thing.**

VIZIER, SNAKE TAMER
**New Lamps for Old!
Trading New Lamps for Old!**

GENIE
Don't trade that lamp!

MOTHER
Oh yes, I'll trade this old thing.

VIZIER
(to Mother)
Ah, madam, you wish to trade in this lamp? I have some lovely new ones.

SNAKE TAMER
(hold out the basket)
Take your pick! They're all beautiful!

SNAKE
Take the whole basssket!

GENIE
Don't do it!

> *The Vizier and Mother trade lamps. Mother keeps the basket.*

VIZIER
It's mine! I did it!

SNAKE TAMER
Um, you had a little help, I think!

VIZIER
Be quiet! I don't need to listen to your endless whining anymore!

SNAKE
How dare you talk to usss like thisss?

VIZIER
You be quiet too! I don't need either of you anymore. I can just wish for whatever I want!

> *The Vizier rubs the lamp.*

SFX: Lamp Magic (Short)

> *The Genie sneaks up behind the Vizier and startles him.*

GENIE
Yes, master?

VIZIER
Ah yes, my own personal Genie, who must obey my every command! Bow, Genie!

GENIE
(bowing reluctantly)
I'm bowing, but I ain't liking it. What is your first wish, master?

VIZIER
First, I wish for that lousy Aladdin to be a poor market brat again.

The Genie claps his/her hands.

SFX: Lamp Magic (Super Short)

GENIE
It is so, master. What is your second wish?

VIZIER
I wish to be immensely rich!

GENIE
Yeah, yeah, that's what everyone wants.

The Genie claps. Assistants appear with chests of jewels.

SFX: Lamp Magic (Short)

GENIE
I hope you don't mind if I use the same jewels as last time. Recycling is a good thing, after all.

The Vizier pushes the lamp at the Snake Tamer while he gleefully runs his hands through the jewels.

VIZIER
I'm rich! I'm rich!

GENIE
Maybe so, but I ain't singing a song for you.

The Guards enter, with Aladdin in custody. His turban and cape are gone.

BURLY
Come one, come all!

SURLY
Come out to see this impostor punished!

The Ensemble, including the Landlord, enters, gossiping avidly.

ENSEMBLE
(ad lib)
An impostor? It's Aladdin! I can't believe it! What did he do?

MOTHER
Oh no!

LANDLORD
I always said that Aladdin would come to a bad end!

CURLY
Make way for the Sultan and Sultaness!

SFX: Fanfare

The Sultan and Sultaness enter.

SULTAN
We can't allow false Princes into the Palace!

SULTANESS
He seemed like such a nice boy, too.

The Princess enters with her Friends.

PRINCESS
Stop! I won't let you punish him!

ALADDIN
I'm sorry, Princess. I never meant to deceive you, honestly.

PRINCESS
I wish I could make things right! I wish, I wish, I wish!

SNAKE TAMER
She wishes? *(to the Snake)* Are you thinking what I'm thinking?

SNAKE
I sssure am!

The Snake Tamer starts sidling over to the Princess. The Vizier looks up.

VIZIER
But you can't fix anything by wishing, Princess. Only I can make wishes that count. And my next wish is to be Sultan!

SULTAN, SULTANESS
What?

LANDLORD
Him as Sultan! Oh no!

VIZIER
Yes, as soon as I—*(reaches for the lamp)* Where did it go? Genie, bring me the lamp!

GENIE
Sorry, fella, but no lamp, no ordering me around.

VIZIER
Where is it? Where is it?

The Vizier searches frantically, but no one will help him.

MOTHER
I don't have it!

LANDLORD
I don't have it!

ENSEMBLE
(ad lib)
Not me! I've never seen it! I don't have it!

The Snake Tamer gives the lamp to the Princess, who holds it up.

PRINCESS
Is this what you're looking for, Vizier?

VIZIER
Give it to me! You don't know how to use it!

ALADDIN
Rub the lamp, Princess!

> *The Princess rubs the lamp. The Genie slides over to her. She can now see him/her.*

SFX: Lamp Magic (short)

GENIE
Yes, master? What is your first wish?

PRINCESS
I wish for the Vizier—

VIZIER
No! Please!

PRINCESS
—to croak like a frog!

> *The Genie claps his/her hands.*

SFX: Lamp Magic (super short)

VIZIER
Ribbit!

> *Everyone laughs.*

LANDLORD
We can't have a frog as Vizier!

ENSEMBLE
(ad lib)
What a fool! He looks like a frog too!

VIZIER
Ribbit!

> *Everyone laughs.*

SULTANESS
Get him out of here!

SULTAN
Guards, throw him in prison.

VIZIER
(sadly)
Ribbit!

> *The Guards take the Vizier offstage.*

SNAKE TAMER
Bye-bye, Vizier!

SNAKE
Good riddanssse!

GENIE
Nice wish, Princess! What's next?

PRINCESS
I wish for Aladdin to be a rich prince again.

> *The Genie claps. The Assistants move the jewels to Aladdin and restore his turban & cape. Everyone cheers.*

SFX: Lamp Magic (Medium)

ALADDIN
Princess!

PRINCESS
Prince Aladdin!

GENIE
What about your third wish, Princess?

PRINCESS
What more could I ask for? I can't think of anything.

GENIE
Well, if you'd like, I have a suggestion...

ALADDIN
What now?

GENIE
The only way to make sure no one evil gets hold of the lamp again is to wish for me to be free.

The Princess and Aladdin look at each other.

GENIE
Please? Pleeeease?

ALADDIN
Seems reasonable to me.

PRINCESS
Then, for my third wish, I wish for the Genie to be free forever!

Music 10: Finale: Rings on Your Fingers
Vocal chorus

The Genie dances. The Sultan and Sultaness greet Aladdin as a son-in-law. Mother hugs the Princess. The Guards return. Genie conducts and all sing.

ALL EXCEPT GENIE
Now I've (he's) got...
Rings on my (his) fingers, (GENIE: WOO!)
Bells on my (his) toes, (GENIE: WOO!)
Elephants to ride upon,
And diamonds, goodness knows!

GENIE
(over the music)
And here's a gift from me, since Aladdin never got his last wish: everyone gets to live happily ever after!

Everyone cheers.

ALL
I'm (He's) the Prince of Mumbo-Jumbo
Jijiboo Jay. OK!

THE END

THE DANCING PRINCESSES AND THE GARDENING BOY

CHARACTERS

Yardley	M	Gardening Boy
Rose	F	Friendly Princess
Queen	F	Exasperated parent
Head Gardener	M or F	Responsible boss
Weedy	M or F	Goofy gardener
Magician	M or F	Scatterbrained wizard
Lobelia	F	Snooty dance-obsessed princesses
Bougainvillea	F	
Agapantha	F	
Chrysanthemum	F	
Azalea	F	**Optional** princesses. Omit the lines of any name not used.
Camellia	F	
Gladiola	F	
Hydrangea	F	
Jacaranda	F	
Oleander	F	
Wisteria	F	
Charming	M	Princes, obsessed with their horses
Valiant	M	
Debonair	M	**Optional** princes. Re-allocate their lines to Charming & Valiant
Intrepid	M	
Buff	M or F	Queen's Guards
Gruff	M or F	

Since the play is not called "The Twelve Dancing Princesses," you can easily omit some of the sisters, down to a minimum of five (Rose, Lobelia, Bougainvillea, Agapantha, Chrysanthemum).

The dancing can be ballroom style for couples, or your actresses can show off their ballet moves.

There should always be fewer Princes than Princesses. The lines labeled Debonair and Intrepid should be assigned to Charming and Valiant if you only have two Princes.

3-5 M, 6-13 F, 5 M or F (Minimum cast size 14, maximum 23)

LENGTH

30 minutes

SCENE

A fairy-tale palace

STRUCTURE

Prologue: Magical Ballroom (Song: *Dancing, Just Dancing*)

Scene 1: Palace Garden (Songs: *Shoes!, Rose, A Princess So Rare*)

Scene 2: Princesses' Room (Song: *Odd Princess Rose*)

Scene 3: Magical Ballroom (Songs: *My Horse Is Better Than Yours, Dancing, Just Dancing*)

Scene 4: Princesses' Room (Song: *Finale: Shoes!*)

THE DANCING PRINCESSES AND THE GARDENING BOY

Prologue

The Magical Ballroom. The Princesses and Princes enter and sing while they're dancing singly or in pairs. The Princesses can "cut in" on each other to dance with a Prince.

Music 01: Dancing, Just Dancing
Tune: And the Band Played On (Palmer and Ward, 1895)
Vocal chorus, half-chorus dance break, vocal half-chorus

PRINCESSES, PRINCES
Dancing, just dancing each night until dawn
While the band plays on.
We glide 'cross the floor seven hours or more
While the band plays on.

LOBELIA, BOUGAINVILLEA
Our shoes are in tatters,

AGAPANTHA, CHRYSANTHEMUM
We don't think it matters.

ROSE
But Mother is filled with alarm!

PRINCESSES, PRINCES
We dance ev'ry night till the dawn's early light,
While the band plays on.

Dance break (half-chorus)

PRINCESSES ONLY
Our shoes are in tatters, we don't think it matters.
But Mother is filled with alarm!

PRINCESSES, PRINCES
We dance ev'ry night till the dawn's early light,
While the band plays on.
How the band plays on!

They all exit dancing.

END OF PROLOGUE

Scene 1: Palace Garden

A few blossoming shrubs. The HEAD GARDENER enters, followed by YARDLEY and WEEDY. Yardley is getting a tour because it's his first day on the job. The Gardener and Weedy are carrying hoes or shovels; Yardley has a basket of daisies.

GARDENER
You'll be working here, Yardley, in the flowerbeds.

YARDLEY
Yes, Head Gardener.

WEEDY
I wish I could work over here with the purty flowers!

GARDENER
No, Weedy, you'll stay in the vegetable garden where you belong.

WEEDY
Yeah, where nobody can see me, cuz I'm funny-looking.

Weedy demonstrates how funny-looking he/she is.

GARDENER
Well, yes, Weedy, you are funny-looking.

YARDLEY
That's okay, Weedy. I probably won't get a lot of visitors in the flower garden either.

WEEDY
Oh yes, you will!

GARDENER
The Queen walks in the flower garden every morning, with all the Princesses.

YARDLEY
So that's why I have this basket! To give flowers to the Princesses!

THE DANCING PRINCESSES AND THE GARDENING BOY

WEEDY
Yeah, I'm soooooo jealous!

The Guards are heard singing offstage.

GUARDS
Oh-ee-oh! Yo-oh!

GARDENER
(looking offstage)
Look, here comes the Queen! Yardley, bow! Weedy, hide!

WEEDY
Yeah, yeah, yeah.

The Head Gardener and Yardley bow. Weedy hides behind a shrub. The QUEEN enters, escorted by the GUARDS.

BUFF
Make way for the Queen!

GRUFF
All bow to Her Majesty!

QUEEN
Greetings, lowly gardeners.

GARDENER
Good morning, Your Majesty.

YARDLEY
I am deeply honored by your presence.

QUEEN
You should be.

WEEDY
(from behind the shrub)
Yeah, I'm honored to be behind this bush.

The Queen and Guards look around to see who is talking.

The Guards move threateningly toward the shrub.

GUARDS
What was that?

GARDENER
Ah, that was just… a cat!

QUEEN
A cat?

WEEDY
(from behind the shrub)
Meow.

GARDENER
See?

The Guards relax.

YARDLEY
(timidly holding out a flower)
Would your Majesty care for a flower?

The Guards move between Yardley and the Queen.

BUFF
Do not approach the Queen!

GRUFF
Stay back, gardening boy!

QUEEN
Oh, those flowers are for my sweet daughters. *(calling offstage)* Lobelia!

LOBELIA enters and reluctantly takes a flower from Yardley.

LOBELIA
Yes, Mother. Eww, he's so dirty!

QUEEN
Bougainvillea!

THE DANCING PRINCESSES AND THE GARDENING BOY

BOUGAINVILLEA enters and reluctantly takes a flower from Yardley.

BOUGAINVILLEA
Yes, Mother. Eww, he'd better not touch me!

QUEEN
Agapantha! Chrysanthemum!

YARDLEY
(quietly, to the Head Gardener)
I don't get it. Why is she calling out flowers?

GARDENER
(quietly to Yardley)
Shh! The Princesses are all named for flowers.

WEEDY
(poking his/her head out, quietly to Yardley)
But they sure ain't as sweet as flowers.

AGAPANTHA and CHRYSANTHEMUM enter and take flowers from Yardley.

AGAPANTHA, CHRYSANTHEMUM
Yes, Mother. Eww, a gardening boy!

QUEEN
Azalea! Camellia! Gladiola! Hydrangea! Jacaranda! Oleander! Wisteria!
Note: Adapt this list to fit your cast. Cut the lines belonging to any omitted Princesses.

The remaining Princesses (except Rose) enter in a giggling group. Each Princess comes forward reluctantly and takes a flower from Yardley.

PRINCESSES
(One by one)
Eww!

QUEEN
Now girls, say thank you.

LOBELIA
To a gardening boy?

BOUGAINVILLEA
Who digs in the dirt?

AGAPANTHA
And pulls the weeds?

CHRYSANTHEMUM
And touches the slimy worms?

PRINCESSES
Never!

The Princesses run off, giggling.

BUFF
Your Majesty, we are still missing one Princess.

GRUFF
The gardening boy has one flower left.

QUEEN
Oh that's right, the one with the strange name I can never remember…
Agapantha? Bougainvillea? No, they were here…

YARDLEY
(to the Head Gardener)
A name that's stranger than Bougainvillea?

QUEEN
Oh I know! (calling offstage) Rose!

YARDLEY
(to the Head Gardener)
Rose is a strange name?

GARDENER
(to Yardley)
Shh!

Rose enters. She is absorbed in a book.

ROSE
Yes, Mother, here I am.

THE DANCING PRINCESSES AND THE GARDENING BOY

QUEEN
Rose, come get your flower!

Rose, absorbed in her book, holds out her hand to Yardley, who puts the flower in it. Rose looks at it with an interest no other princess has shown.

ROSE
Oh look, it's a *Bellis perennis*!

QUEEN
Oh Rose, stop using those big words!

ROSE
Sorry, Mother. *(to Yardley)* But this *Bellis perennis* is lovely!

YARDLEY
Oh, you know the flower's Latin name!

GARDENER
Yes, she's the only Princess who does.

ROSE
(to Yardley)
Do you work here in the flower garden?

YARDLEY
I do from now on.

ROSE
Maybe I can come help you sometime.

WEEDY
(poking his/her head out)
You can help me in the vegetable garden whenever you want!

GARDENER
(pushing Weedy's head back behind the shrub)
Shh!

QUEEN
Princesses don't work in gardens anyway.

ROSE
Maybe <u>Princesses</u> don't, but <u>I</u> still want to.

213

*Lobelia, Bougainvillea,
Agapantha and
Chrysanthemum run in and
grab Rose's arms.*

LOBELIA
Rose! Come with us to get new shoes!

QUEEN
Your shoes look fine to me.

BOUGAINVILLEA
These are for walking! Our dancing slippers are all tattered!

*Bougainvillea holds up a pair of
ragged ballet slippers.*

QUEEN
Oh, very well.

AGAPANTHA
Rose! Let's go shoe-shopping!

CHRYSANTHEMUM
C'mon, Rose! You always choose the best ones!

*Rose looks back over her
shoulder as the Princesses pull
her offstage.*

ROSE
I'm sorry, Mother, but our slippers really are all worn out…

The Queen is exasperated.

Music 02: Shoes!
Tune: Ja-Da (Carleton, 1918)
Vocal chorus

QUEEN
Shoes!

GUARDS
Shoes!

QUEEN
Shoes!

THE DANCING PRINCESSES AND THE GARDENING BOY

GUARDS
Shoes!

QUEEN
**Every day they want new shoes!
Shoes!**

GUARDS
Shoes!

QUEEN
Shoes!

GUARDS
Shoes!

QUEEN
**I have got the new-shoe blues!
Every night I lock up all the windows and doors,
Every morn they look as if they've been in the wars.
Shoes!**

GUARDS
Shoes!

QUEEN
Shoes!

GUARDS
Shoes!

QUEEN
Every day they want new—

GUARDS
Every day they want new—

QUEEN, GUARDS
Every day they want new shoes!

QUEEN
(shouting to end the song)
Shoes!
(muttering as she exits)
Shoes, shoes, shoes!

*The Queen and Guards exit.
The Guards are heard singing
offstage.*

GUARDS
Oh-ee-oh! Yo-oh!

*Weedy comes out from behind
the shrub.*

YARDLEY
Boy, she seems really frustrated!

WEEDY
You'd be frustrated too if you had that bunch for daughters.

GARDENER
Except for Princess Rose.

YARDLEY
(dreamily)
Yeah, she's different.

Music 03: Rose, A Princess So Rare
Tune: Rose of Washington Square (Hanley, 1920)
Vocal chorus

YARDLEY
Rose, a princess so rare
I'm walking on air
Because you talked right to me!
Rose!

WEEDY, GARDENER
He's got it bad!

YARDLEY
Your nature did not mean,

WEEDY, GARDENER
For you to stay unseen,

YARDLEY
But be the queen

YARDLEY, WEEDY, GARDENER
Of our fair garden!

THE DANCING PRINCESSES AND THE GARDENING BOY

YARDLEY
Rose!

WEEDY, GARDENER
Our Princess Rose!

YARDLEY
You're not like the rest,

WEEDY, GARDENER
No thorns on Rose!

YARDLEY
You're clearly the best

WEEDY, GARDENER
Yes, you're the best!

YARDLEY
Beyond compare!

WEEDY, GARDENER
Beyond compare!

YARDLEY
Bring on the sun that shines for you, only you,

WEEDY, GARDENER
And make the flowers all sparkle with dew!

YARDLEY
Oh Rose!

WEEDY, GARDENER
Dear Princess Rose!

YARDLEY
A Princess so rare!

WEEDY, GARDENER
A rose so rare!

WEEDY
I know someone with a crush on a Princess!

GARDENER
Aw, be quiet, Weedy. Let's get back to work.

*The Gardener and Weedy exit.
Yardley examines the shrubs.
Suddenly, the MAGICIAN
enters, with a puff of smoke or a
lighting effect.*

MAGICIAN
(waving his/her magic wand)
Ta-da! Here I am!

YARDLEY
Who are you?

MAGICIAN
Oh, just your friendly local wizard.

YARDLEY
A wizard?

MAGICIAN
Sure, watch this. Hocus-pocus!

*The Magician waves his/her
magic wand. Nothing happens.*

MAGICIAN
(continued)
Hmm, that always worked before… Okay, watch this. Abracadabra!

*The Magician waves his/her
magic wand. Nothing happens.*

MAGICIAN
(continued)
Oh, never mind. I'm here, and that's all that matters.

YARDLEY
What do you want with me?

MAGICIAN
I'm here to make you happy… AND the Queen… AND Princess Rose.

YARDLEY
Wow, that's a lot of happiness. What do I have to do?

THE DANCING PRINCESSES AND THE GARDENING BOY

MAGICIAN
Take this cloak. It will make you invisible to everyone in the palace.

The Magician hands a cloak to Yardley, who holds it up so we can see it has no hood.

YARDLEY
How can a cloak like this hide my whole body? Won't people see my head and feet?

MAGICIAN
(exasperated)
Never you mind how it works. It's <u>magic</u>!

YARDLEY
Okay, but why do I want to be invisible?

MAGICIAN
That way you can follow the Princesses and find out how they wear out their shoes every night.

YARDLEY
How will that make me happy?

MAGICIAN
The Queen has offered a reward for whoever solves the mystery. Won't that make you happy?

YARDLEY
Well, yeah. How will that make Princess Rose happy?

MAGICIAN
She hates keeping secrets from her mother. She'll be so glad to have the truth come out!

YARDLEY
Okay! I'll do it!

MAGICIAN
I should warn you that several Princes have tried before, and have never been seen again.

YARDLEY
Oh. That's bad.

MAGICIAN
But they didn't have a super-duper invisibility cloak like you will.

YARDLEY
That's okay then. I'll try it tonight! Thanks!

Yardley exits. The Magician is alone onstage.

MAGICIAN
He doesn't realize that I'm only helping him for Rose's sake. She and I are good friends, ever since I taught her to read.

Music 04: Reprise: Rose, A Princess So Rare
Vocal half-chorus

MAGICIAN
You bring new meaning to the books I adore,
And make me see things like never before!
Oh Rose! A princess so rare!

The Magician waves his/her wand and exits, with a puff of smoke or a lighting effect.

END OF SCENE 1

THE DANCING PRINCESSES AND THE GARDENING BOY

Scene 2: Princesses' Room

Vanity table with seat. Full-length mirrors (rolling or imagined on the "fourth wall"). One exit leads into the palace and the other is a "secret door" that leads through a maze to the Magical Ballroom.

Rose is seated at the vanity. The other Princesses are drifting around the room.

LOBELIA
These new slippers make me feel like I'm floating!

PRINCESSES
(ad lib)
Me too! I'm light as a feather! I'm going to dance better than ever!

ROSE
I feel so wrong about this secret dancing. And I feel sorry for those poor Princes!

BOUGAINVILLEA
Poor? They're lucky to be dancing with us instead of arguing about their stupid horses all the time.

ROSE
I still think I ought to tell Mother.

AGAPANTHA
Don't you dare, Rose!

CHRYSANTHEMUM
You promised that you would never tell her!

ROSE
(sighing)
Yes, I did, and I always keep my promises.

The Guards are heard singing offstage.

GUARDS
Oh-ee-oh! Yo-oh!

PRINCESSES
(ad lib)
Shh! Here she comes!

> *The Queen enters, followed by the Guards and Yardley in his invisibility cloak. He lingers upstage and dodges any Guards or Princesses who come near him.*

Note: The audience can see Yardley, of course, but no one onstage looks at him.

> *The Guards check the room to make sure there are no intruders.*

QUEEN
Are you all ready for bed, girls?

PRINCESSES
(fake-yawning)
Almost, Mother!

LOBELIA
(fake-yawning)
I'm soooo sleepy!

BOUGAINVILLEA
(fake-yawning)
I can't wait for lights out!

BUFF
All clear over here, Your Majesty.

ROSE
Yes, we're all alone in here, Mother.

GRUFF
All clear over here as well, Your Majesty.

PRINCESSES
(fake-yawning)
Goodnight, Mother!

QUEEN
Well, goodnight girls. I'll lock the door as usual.

THE DANCING PRINCESSES AND THE GARDENING BOY

> *The Queen and Guards exit.*
> *The Guards are heard singing*
> *offstage.*

GUARDS
Oh-ee-oh! Yo-oh!

AGAPANTHA
She's gone!

PRINCESSES
Yay!

CHRYSANTHEMUM
Let's get ready!

PRINCESSES
Yay!

> *The Princesses rush to put on*
> *their dress-up accessories,*
> *giggling and preening themselves*
> *in front of the mirrors.*

PRINCESSES
(ad lib)
See my new tiara? Move aside, it's my turn at the mirror! Let me look! I love this new fan!

> *Rose is still sitting at the vanity.*

ROSE
I don't know why I'm not excited about dancing tonight.

LOBELIA
Well, Rose, you are a bit… odd.

BOUGAINVILLEA
Different!

AGAPANTHA
Strange!

AZALEA
Unusual!

CAMELLIA
Weird!

GLADIOLA
Bizarre!

HYDRANGEA
Peculiar!

JACARANDA
Unconventional!

OLEANDER
Offbeat!

WISTERIA
Eccentric!

CHRYSANTHEMUM
In other words, you're…

PRINCESSES
…not like us!

ROSE
(sighing)
No, I'm not like you.

The Princesses gather around Rose.

Music 05: Odd Princess Rose
Tune: Second Hand Rose (Hanley, 1921)
Vocal chorus

ROSE
You might call me Odd Princess Rose

PRINCESSES
That's right, you're "Odd Princess Rose."

ROSE
Why I'm so diff'rent, nobody knows.
Mother says I shouldn't be so wordy.

PRINCESSES
Reading all those books has made you nerdy!

THE DANCING PRINCESSES AND THE GARDENING BOY

ROSE
Odd Princess Rose

PRINCESSES
You're such an odd princess, Rose.

ROSE
I love to dance, but not as much as you.

AGAPANTHA
(spoken)
We do love to dance!

ROSE
**Even when I'm dancing with Prince Charming, I fear
Mother will be hurt when the deception comes clear.**

CHRYSANTHEMUM
(spoken)
Who's going to tell her?

ROSE
Odd Princess Rose

PRINCESSES
We think you're odd, Princess Rose.

ROSE
What's odd is how I love to dance!

PRINCESSES
That's not odd!

> *Yardley has crept closer during the song, and now has to jump out of the way as the Princesses start to leave.*

LOBELIA
Let's go!

PRINCESSES
Yay!

BOUGAINVILLEA
Lobelia, you lead us through the maze tonight.

LOBELIA
Everybody, follow me out through the secret door!

PRINCESSES
Yay!

> *The Princesses, humming, follow Lobelia off.*

> **Music 06: Dancing, Just Dancing Humming Exit 1**
> **Vocal chorus (fade out as needed)**

> *Rose stands up and bumps into Yardley, or he steps on her dress.*

ROSE
(over the music)
What was that? Is someone in the room with us?

BOUGAINVILLEA
Oh Rose, you're just imagining things again. C'mon!

> *Bougainvillea exits, followed by Rose and then Yardley. The Princesses continue humming during the scene change.*

END OF SCENE 2

THE DANCING PRINCESSES AND THE GARDENING BOY

Scene 3: Magical Ballroom

Fancy curtains, a few gilt chairs. A nice touch would be potted gold, silver and "diamond" trees as in the fairy tale. One exit leads to a dining room and the other leads back to the palace.

The PRINCES enter from the dining room, in the middle of a ridiculous argument that has obviously been going on for a long time.

CHARMING
No, Valiant, <u>my</u> horse is better, because he is an even gold color all over.

VALIANT
No, Charming, <u>my</u> horse is better, because he has the longest, silkiest tail.

DEBONAIR
<u>My</u> horse has the biggest brownest eyes!

INTREPID
<u>My</u> horse can neigh the loudest!

ALL PRINCES
(ad lib)
<u>My</u> horse! No, <u>my</u> horse! Mine's the best! Mine! No, mine! Mine!

Each Prince yells about the virtues of his own horse, then falls into a sulk because no one is listening.

**Music 07: *My Horse Is Better Than Yours*
Tune: *Oh, You Beautiful Doll* (Brown and Ayer, 1911)
Vocal chorus**

ALL PRINCES
**I have told you before,
My horse is better than yours!**

CHARMING, DEBONAIR
I don't want to hear about it!

VALIANT, INTREPID
Why d'ya have to go and shout it?

ALL PRINCES
I have told you before,
A thousand times or more:
If you'd seen how high my horse can jump the bar,
You'd have to say that he's the best by far!

CHARMING
Mine!

VALIANT
Mine!

DEBONAIR
Mine!

INTREPID
Mine!

ALL PRINCES
Mine is better than yours!

The Princes sulk.

CHARMING
(looking offstage)
Oh, here come the Princesses.

VALIANT
It's time to face the music and dance.

DEBONAIR
I call dibs on Rose!

INTREPID
Rose is going to dance with me first!

ALL PRINCES
(ad lib)
No, me! Me! She likes me best! No, me!

The Princes are arguing as the Princesses enter. Lobelia leads, with Bougainvillea and Rose trailing, followed by Yardley.

THE DANCING PRINCESSES AND THE GARDENING BOY

Yardley lingers upstage, but has to frequently dodge to avoid the others.

LOBELIA
Are you boys fighting?

BOUGAINVILLEA
Not over those horses again!

AGAPANTHA
Maybe they're arguing about who gets to dance with me first!

PRINCESSES
(ad lib)
Or me? They want to dance with me! Me!

CHRYSANTHEMUM
No, it's my turn to get a Prince for the first dance!

PRINCESSES
(ad lib)
No it isn't! It's my turn! Mine!

ROSE
Oh for goodness' sake! We sound just as silly as they do with their endless horse argument!

PRINCESSES
(ad lib)
No we don't! How can you say such a thing? We are not silly!

CHARMING
Would you care to dance with me, Princess Rose?

ROSE
No, thank you.

VALIANT
Maybe you'd prefer to dance with me?

ROSE
No, I'll just sit this one out.

Rose sits down.

DEBONAIR
What about you, Princess Lobelia?

LOBELIA
I'd love to!

INTREPID
Will you do me the honor, Princess Bougainvillea?

BOUGAINVILLEA
Of course!

> *Everyone else partners up as far as possible.*

PRINCESSES
(ad lib)
Let's dance now! I'm ready! What are we waiting for?

> *Everyone dances except Rose. Princesses who don't have a Prince either dance singly or in pairs with each other, or can "cut in" on each other to get their chance to dance with a Prince. Yardley tries to get closer to Rose, but has to keep dodging the dancers.*
>
> *The choreography can be the same as in the Prologue, except that Rose sits this one out.*

Music 08: Reprise: Dancing, Just Dancing
Vocal chorus, half-chorus dance break, vocal half-chorus

PRINCESSES, PRINCES
Dancing, just dancing each night until dawn
While the band plays on.
We glide 'cross the floor seven hours or more
While the band plays on.

LOBELIA, BOUGAINVILLEA
Our shoes are in tatters,

AGAPANTHA, CHRYSANTHEMUM
We don't think it matters.

THE DANCING PRINCESSES AND THE GARDENING BOY

ROSE
But Mother is filled with alarm!

PRINCESSES, PRINCES
**We dance ev'ry night till the dawn's early light,
While the band plays on.**

Dance break (half-chorus)

PRINCESSES ONLY
**Our shoes are in tatters, we don't think it matters.
But Mother is filled with alarm!**

PRINCESSES, PRINCES
**We dance ev'ry night till the dawn's early light,
While the band plays on.
How the band plays on!**

CHARMING
I believe it is time for refreshments!

VALIANT
Can we interest you ladies in a glass of punch? Or some cake?

PRINCESSES
(ad lib)
Ooh, yes! I'm dying for some punch! All this dancing really makes me thirsty! Those little cakes are so yummy!

Everyone starts to exit except Rose and Yardley. Agapantha and Chrysanthemum linger onstage for a moment.

AGAPANTHA
Rose, what's the matter with you? You've been sitting there for hours!

ROSE
I've had a funny feeling all night, like someone is staring at me.

Yardley realizes he's been staring and awkwardly looks away.

CHRYSANTHEMUM
Oh Rose, you have such a wild imagination!

*Agapantha and
Chrysanthemum giggle and exit.
Yardley sneaks up right behind
where Rose is sitting.*

YARDLEY
Princess Rose?

ROSE
(startled)
Who's that?

Yardley removes his cloak.

YARDLEY
It's Yardley, the gardening boy.

ROSE
Oh, it's you! How did you get here?

YARDLEY
A Magician gave me this cloak and told me to follow the Princesses.

ROSE
Oh, what a good idea! That Magician is so smart!

YARDLEY
Nobody realized I was here, except you.

ROSE
Are you going to follow us back, and tell the Queen?

YARDLEY
Yes, but I think I should take those Princes back with me for proof.

ROSE
Oh yes, please take them home so they can see their horses again! *(suddenly doubtful)* But my sisters will see you as we go through the maze.

YARDLEY
Is there some way you can mark the path, so we can stay further back?

Laughter from offstage.

ROSE
Oh dear, here they come! Put your cloak back on!

THE DANCING PRINCESSES AND THE GARDENING BOY

Yardley puts on his cloak.

YARDLEY
But the maze—

ROSE
Ssh! They'll hear you! I'll think of something!

The Princesses and Princes return. Lobelia is carrying a cake or pastry for Rose.

LOBELIA
Here, Rose, I brought you a cake for the trip home.

ROSE
Oh, is it time to go back?

BOUGAINVILLEA
Yes. Our shoes are done for the night!

AGAPANTHA
They're tattered!

CHRYSANTHEMUM
Not to mention worn out!

AZALEA
Torn!

CAMELLIA
Holey!

GLADIOLA
Frayed!

HYDRANGEA
Ragged!

JACARANDA
Beat-up!

OLEANDER
Useless!

WISTERIA
Ruined!

ROSE
(with emphasis)
I'll eat this cake on the way. It's so CRUMBLY! I bet I'll leave a TRAIL OF CRUMBS all the way HOME!

> *Yardley visibly "gets" what Rose is saying and touches her sleeve to let her know he understands.*

ROSE
We'd better get going then.

CHARMING
Farewell, dear Princesses!

VALIANT
Parting is such sweet sorrow!

PRINCESSES
(ad lib)
Good night! Sweet dreams! Until tomorrow!

> *The Princesses, humming, exit.*

Music 09: Dancing, Just Dancing Humming Exit 2
Vocal chorus (fade out as needed)

> *Rose exits last, deliberately dropping some cake crumbs. Yardley watches her closely, then turns his attention to the Princes.*

DEBONAIR
(over the music)
Well, let's go finish the refreshments!

INTREPID
While we're doing that, I have a few things to tell you about my horse...

> *The Princes groan and exit. Yardley follows. The Princesses continue humming during the scene change.*

END OF SCENE 3

THE DANCING PRINCESSES AND THE GARDENING BOY

Scene 4: Princesses' Room

Same as Scene 2. The Princesses are just entering through the "secret door."

PRINCESSES
(ad lib)
Ooh, I'm sleepy! I'm ready for a nap! What a great night that was!

LOBELIA
(really yawning)
Now for a few hours of sleep!

BOUGAINVILLEA
(really yawning)
Until Mother takes us on our walk through the garden!

Rose enters last, brushing the last crumbs from her hands.

ROSE
We're running late this morning. Mother may be here any minute.

The Guards are heard singing offstage.

GUARDS
(offstage)
Oh-ee-oh! Yo-oh!

PRINCESSES
(ad lib)
Uh-oh! It's her! She's here! Quick, put away our finery!

The Princesses start frantically removing their accessories, but it's too late. The Queen enters, followed by the Guards.

QUEEN
Good morni—hey, what are you girls up to?

AGAPANTHA
(pretending innocence)
We all woke up early!

CHRYSANTHEMUM
(pretending innocence)
Isn't that funny?

PRINCESSES
(ad lib)
It's great to get up so early! We just love this time of day! Oh, what a beautiful morning!

QUEEN
(suspiciously)
Let me see your shoes! If they're tattered, I want to know the reason why.

> *The Princesses shift guiltily, but before they can respond, Yardley enters from the secret door. He is still wearing his cloak.*

YARDLEY
I know the reason why, Your Majesty.

> *Everyone looks around to see who is talking. The Guards cross their spears to protect the Queen. The Princesses are amazed.*

BUFF
Who was that?

GRUFF
Stand back, whoever you are!

> *Yardley removes his cloak. Everyone reacts as if they can now see him.*

BUFF
It's that gardening boy!

PRINCESSES
(ad lib)
Where'd he come from? How dare he come into our room? He's sure got a lot of nerve! What a spy!

QUEEN
Guards, arrest that gardener! Throw him in the dungeon!

THE DANCING PRINCESSES AND THE GARDENING BOY

GRUFF
All right you, come with us.

The Guards grab Yardley by the arms and begin to drag him away.

YARDLEY
Wait! I can explain everything! Just ask the Magician!

QUEEN
The Magician? You mean that bizarre wizard?

The Magician enters, with a puff of smoke or a lighting effect.

MAGICIAN
(waving his/her magic wand)
Did someone mention me?

YARDLEY
Tell them what you told me to do!

MAGICIAN
Who, me?

ROSE
Now don't tease us, Magician. After all, where else did that invisibility cloak come from?

MAGICIAN
Oh yes, that was me. *(to the Queen)* You don't need to arrest him.

QUEEN
(reluctantly, to the Guards)
Very well, let him go.

GUARDS
(disappointed)
Yes, Your Majesty.

The Guards release Yardley.

QUEEN
(to the Guards)
Go fetch the Head Gardener, so he/she can hear what this gardening boy has been up to.

GUARDS
Yes, Your Majesty.

The Guards exit.

QUEEN
All right, somebody needs to start talking, and fast.

YARDLEY
(at the same time as the Magician)
It was like this—

MAGICIAN
(at the same time as Yardley)
Well you see—

QUEEN
One at a time! You, gardening boy!

MAGICIAN
Over to you, Yardley. You're the hero of this story.

YARDLEY
I followed the Princesses last night—

LOBELIA
Followed us where? We were asleep, weren't we, girls?

PRINCESSES
(ad lib)
Yes we were! We slept like logs!

ROSE
Oh, let him finish!

YARDLEY
They went out a secret door and through a maze to a magical ballroom—

BOUGAINVILLEA
That's a fine story! Prove it, gardening boy!

PRINCESSES
(ad lib)
He's a liar! We were asleep! There's no proof!

QUEEN
Can you prove it, gardening boy?

THE DANCING PRINCESSES AND THE GARDENING BOY

ROSE
Even if you don't believe a gardening boy, would you believe a Prince?

QUEEN
A Prince? What Prince?

YARDLEY
Come in, Your Highnesses!

The Princes enter from the secret door.

QUEEN
Why, those are the Princes I sent along to figure out the secret of the tattered slippers!
(to the Princes)
What happened to you?

CHARMING
We've been dancing in the magical ballroom ever since.

VALIANT
The Princesses are such passionate dancers!

DEBONAIR
We've missed our horses, though.

INTREPID
We only followed this gardening boy because he promised to take us to the stables.

ROSE
I think your horses have been missing you, too. You know I visit them every afternoon

PRINCES
(ad lib)
You do? How's my noble steed? Is he lonely?

The Guards enter with the Head Gardener, with Weedy following.

GARDENER
(bowing)
You sent for me, Your Majesty?

WEEDY
(bowing)
You didn't send for me, Your Majesty, but I'm here anyway.

QUEEN
What do you mean, Gardener, by letting your assistant spy on the Princesses?

GARDENER
Yardley was spying? I didn't know.

WEEDY
Ooh, can I be a spy too? Huh? Huh?

GARDENER, YARDLEY
(to Weedy)
No.

WEEDY
Oh.

ROSE
(to the Queen)
But you shouldn't be angry with Yardley!

MAGICIAN
(to the Queen)
You should reward him for solving the mystery!

QUEEN
Oh you're right, I should. I was going to make the reward a new horse—

PRINCES
(excited)
Ooh!

QUEEN
But that was before I realized that all the Princes would be failures.

PRINCES
(disappointed)
Oh!

QUEEN
So what kind of reward do I give to a gardening boy?

MAGICIAN
I don't know. A crystal ball?

THE DANCING PRINCESSES AND THE GARDENING BOY

GARDENER
A new shovel?

PRINCESSES
Dancing lessons?

PRINCES
Riding lessons?

GUARDS
Fighting lessons?

WEEDY
Banjo lessons?

ALL EXCEPT WEEDY
(to Weedy)
No.

WEEDY
Oh.

ROSE
Why don't you ask Yardley what he wants?

QUEEN
That's an original idea. *(to Yardley)* So, Yardley, what would you like for a reward?

AGAPANTHA
Wait a second! Why should he get a reward for ruining our fun?

CHRYSANTHEMUM
Yeah, we won't be able to go dancing anymore!

QUEEN
We've got a ballroom right here in the castle. You can dance there.

LOBELIA
But you only let us dance there once a month!

BOUGAINVILLEA
We want to dance every night!

PRINCESSES
(ad lib)
We love to dance! Once a month is not enough!

QUEEN
But I can't afford to keep buying you new shoes every day!

MAGICIAN
Is <u>that</u> the main problem? Sheesh, you should have called me! Abracadabra!

> *The Magician waves his/her magic wand. The Princesses react.*

PRINCESSES
(ad lib)
Ooh, my feet! That tingles!

AGAPANTHA
Look, my slippers are new again!

CHRYSANTHEMUM
It's just like magic!

MAGICIAN
Hello, it <u>is</u> magic. Those shoes will never wear out, so you can dance every night.

LOBELIA
But who will we dance with?

BOUGAINVILLEA
(to the Princes)
Will you come dance with us?

AGAPANTHA
Please?

CHRYSANTHEMUM
Pretty please?

CHARMING
I don't know… I'm kinda tired of dancing.

VALIANT
There are lots of other things I'd rather do.

ROSE
(shyly)
If you come dance with us, you can ride your horses over here in a race <u>every night</u>!

THE DANCING PRINCESSES AND THE GARDENING BOY

DEBONAIR
A race! My horse will win!

INTREPID
You just wait! I'll be the first one here every time!

PRINCES
(ad lib)
Me! No, me! My horse will win!

ROSE
(to the Queen)
Well, that takes care of the dancing. Can we get back to Yardley now?

QUEEN
(to Yardley)
So what do you want for your reward?

YARDLEY
I think what I'd like best is to be Head Gardener.

GARDENER
Hey, what about me?

MAGICIAN
You can come work for me. I've got a whole bunch of magical plants growing wild.

GARDENER
Sounds interesting. I'm in!

QUEEN
(to Yardley)
Very well, you are now Head Gardener.

WEEDY
Oh fine. Everyone gets a promotion except me.

YARDLEY
Weedy, I hereby name you the Vegetable Virtuoso.

WEEDY
Virtuoso! Virt-u-o-so! Well, don't I feel special?!

YARDLEY
(to Rose)
I also have an opening for an assistant flower gardener…

ROSE
That'll be me!

YARDLEY
After all, every garden needs a Rose!

Rose and Yardley hold hands.

MAGICIAN
Seems like a happy ending for everyone!

QUEEN
And no more new shoes!

Music 10: Finale: Shoes
Vocal chorus

QUEEN, MAGICIAN
Shoes!

GUARDS, WEEDY, GARDENER
Shoes!

QUEEN, MAGICIAN
Shoes!

GUARDS, WEEDY, GARDENER
Shoes!

PRINCESSES
Now we'll dance in magic shoes!

QUEEN, MAGICIAN
Shoes!

GUARDS, WEEDY, GARDENER
Shoes!

QUEEN, MAGICIAN
Shoes!

GUARDS, WEEDY, GARDENER
Shoes!

PRINCES
(bragging)
My horse never needs new shoes!

THE DANCING PRINCESSES AND THE GARDENING BOY

ROSE, YARDLEY
Working in the garden with the beautiful flow'rs,
We will wear our Wellingtons* for hours and hours.
*Or "gar'dning boots"

QUEEN, MAGICIAN
Shoes!

GUARDS, WEEDY, GARDENER
Shoes!

QUEEN, MAGICIAN
Shoes!

GUARDS, WEEDY, GARDENER
Shoes!

QUEEN, MAGICIAN, ROSE, YARDLEY
Nobody will need new—

GUARDS, WEEDY, GARDENER, PRINCESSES, PRINCES
Nobody will need new—

ALL
Nobody will need new shoes!
(shouted)
Shoes!

THE END

THE SECRET GARDEN
Based on the book by Frances Hodgson Burnett

CHARACTERS (in order of appearance)

The Secret Garden (lines labeled Garden 1 to 5)	M or F	At least 5 actors (up to 55 with solo lines) narrate the action and transform from a sad, dead garden to a blooming paradise
Mary	F	Sulky girl; the only actor who does not double as the Garden
Mrs. Medlock	F	Stern housekeeper
Martha	F	Friendly maid
Mr. Craven	M	Sad, lame father
Ben	M	Surly gardener, funny
Robin	M or F	Perky bird (referred to as he whether played by boy or girl)
Dickon	M	Friendly local lad, Martha's brother
Colin Craven	M	Sulky rich boy; starts in a wheelchair but learns to walk

4 M, 3 F, 6 M or F (plus up to 50 additional M or F with solo lines)

Everyone except Mary doubles as part of the most important role, the Secret Garden. When it is time to play their individual role, the actors retrieve a distinctive costume piece or prop from the Prop Box.

When a line is labeled GARDEN A1, B4, C3 etc., it may be assigned to any actor. However, when a line is labeled GARDEN/MEDLOCK, for example, it belongs to the actor who plays Mrs. Medlock, as she is putting on her distinctive costume piece.

When a line is labeled MRS. MEDLOCK, the actor should already have her distinctive costume piece or prop and be in character.

THE SECRET GARDEN

SET

Misselthwaite Manor, Yorkshire, England

The stage is bare except for a large box and some chairs. All the props and costume pieces are in the box at the start of the show.

The back curtains are closed until the finale. The front curtains are open throughout. The back curtains hide a backdrop painted with colorful flowers and greenery (does not need to be realistic).

Mary is the only character to leave the stage. Other characters move upstage to sit on the floor or chairs with the rest of the Garden.

LENGTH

30 minutes

The Play

The stage is empty. The SECRET GARDEN actors (everyone except Mary) drift on, dressed in dull brown, gray and black, and assemble center stage.

Music 01: Lost and Forgotten
Tune: Beautiful Dreamer (Stephen Foster, 1864)
Vocal chorus, fadeout underscoring

ALL
Lost and forgotten,
Waiting for Spring.
Here in the garden we sorrow and sing.
Weedy and broken,
Hidden by walls,
Oh, how we'll listen when somebody calls.
A secret garden,
Locked by a key.
Nobody comes by to set the flow'rs free.
Lost and forgotten,
Waiting for Spring.
Here in the garden we sorrow and sing.
Here in the garden we sorrow and sing.

The music continues as the Garden actors step forward.

GARDEN A1
This is the story of a garden…

GARDEN A2
A garden that died…

GARDEN A3
And came back to life again.

GARDEN A4
It's also the story of the girl who learned to love the garden.

GARDEN A5
And to love other people as well.

THE SECRET GARDEN

The music fades out. MARY, a sulky girl in a dress and pinafore, enters.

MARY
A little girl had lived in India all her life.

GARDEN B1
Her name was Mary.

GARDEN B2
Mary's parents died in India.

GARDEN B3
Mary didn't have many relatives.

GARDEN B4
Mary came to England to live with her uncle.

GARDEN B5
Mary wasn't happy about it.

MARY
I don't like this country.

GARDEN/ MEDLOCK
The housekeeper went to get Mary from the train.

MRS. MEDLOCK puts on her distinctive costume piece and gets a small suitcase. Mary follows her, looking sulky.

MRS. MEDLOCK
Here we are at your uncle's manor.

GARDEN C1
The manor was a grand big place in a gloomy way.

GARDEN C2
There were almost a hundred rooms in it, though most were shut up and locked.

GARDEN C3
It was six hundred years old and on the edge of the moor.

GARDEN C4
The moor was a great stretch of land covered with heather.

GARDEN C5
To Mary, the moor looked like an endless, dull, purplish sea.

MARY
I don't like it.

> *The actors move upstage, except for Mary, Martha and Medlock.*

MRS. MEDLOCK
It doesn't matter if you like it or not.

MARY
I don't want to stay here.

MRS. MEDLOCK
Well, live on the moors by yourself then! Nobody else wanted you when your parents died.

MARY
(looking at Mrs. Medlock)
I don't like <u>you</u>.

MRS. MEDLOCK
Humph!

GARDEN/ MARTHA
They went into the house.

> *MARTHA, a cheerful maidservant, puts on her distinctive costume piece.*

MRS. MEDLOCK
This is Martha, who will bring your meals.

MARTHA
Yes, Mrs. Medlock. Good morning, Miss Mary.

MARY
I don't like you either.

MRS. MEDLOCK
That's not a nice way to talk.

MARTHA
It's hard to like someone who talks like that.

> *Music 02: I Don't Care A*
> *Tune: I Don't Care (Sutton and Lenox, 1905)*
> *Vocal Chorus, Interlude, Half-chorus*

MARY
I don't care! I don't care!
If people don't like me.
I know that I'm grouchy, unhappy and slouchy,
As sulky as can be.
I don't care! I don't care!
If I do get that mean and stony stare,
No one can amaze me,
Dislike cannot daze me,
'Cause I don't care!

MEDLOCK & MARTHA
They say she's sullen, got no sense.

MARY
I don't care.

MEDLOCK & MARTHA
They may or may not mean offense.

MARY
I don't care.

MEDLOCK & MARTHA
You see, she's sort of independent,
Of a snooty race descendant
No one will be her attendant.

MARY
That's why I don't care!

MARY, MEDLOCK & MARTHA
I don't care! I don't care! (She won't care)
If I do (she does) get that mean and stony stare,
No one can amaze me (her),
Dislike cannot daze me (her)

MARY
'Cause I don't care!

MRS. MEDLOCK
I must go. Martha, make sure she doesn't wander into the—you know.

MARTHA
Yes, Mrs. Medlock.

Mrs. Medlock puts the suitcase back in the box and joins the Garden group. Martha and Mary stare at each other.

MARTHA
Well, Miss Mary, are you hungry?

MARY
No. The you-know-<u>what</u>?

MARTHA
Shall I fetch you a book?

MARY
No. The you-know-<u>what</u>?

MARTHA
Do you want any toys from your case?

MARY
No! What was she talking about? *(stamping her foot)* Tell me now!

MARTHA
A bad temper won't get you what you want.

GARDEN/ CRAVEN
Mary's uncle was usually traveling, but today he was home.

MR. CRAVEN, a sad man who walks with a pronounced limp, picks up his cane and comes downstage. Mrs. Medlock follows.

MARTHA
Oh Mr. Craven, we didn't expect you.

MR. CRAVEN
I'm only here for today. Is this Mary?

MARY
Yes. Are you my uncle?

MR. CRAVEN
Yes. I'm not a very good uncle, though.

MRS. MEDLOCK
(to Mary)
Say thank-you for letting you live here.

MARY
(ungraciously)
Thank you, I suppose.

> *It's obvious Mr. Craven doesn't know what to say to her.*

MR. CRAVEN
Well, be a good girl. *(to Martha)* Don't let her go into the—you know.

MARTHA
Yes, Mr. Craven.

> *Mr. Craven puts his cane in the box and joins the Garden group. Mary is burning with curiosity.*

MARY
What does he mean by you know? Tell me or I'll scream!

MRS. MEDLOCK
Go ahead, tell her.

Music 03: Lost and Forgotten Underscore

MARTHA
One of the gardens is locked up. No one has been in it for ten years.

MARY
Ooh! Why?

MARTHA
Mr. Craven had it closed up when his wife died there. It was her garden.

MARY
Ooh!

MRS. MEDLOCK
He locked the door and buried the key.

MARY
Ooh!

MRS. MEDLOCK
So stay away from the walled garden, or there will be trouble.

> *The music ends. Mrs. Medlock puts her costume piece in the box and joins the Garden group.*

GARDEN/COLIN
Martha and Mary were staring at each other when suddenly…

> *COLIN (in the Garden Group) lets out a moaning wail.*

GARDEN/COLIN
(continued)
Aaaaaaaaaaaaaaaah!

MARY
(startled)
What was that?

MARTHA
Never you mind, Miss Mary.

MARY
It sounded like a person crying.

MARTHA
It must have been the wind blowing across the moor.

GARDEN/COLIN
Aaaaaaaaaaaaaaaah!

MARY
There it is again.

MARTHA
It's the wind, I tell you. Now go and play.

> *Martha puts her distinctive costume piece in the box and*

THE SECRET GARDEN

> *joins the Garden group as they come forward.*

GARDEN D1
Mary had nothing better to do, so she wandered outside.

> *Mary exits.*

GARDEN D2
The manor had great gardens, with wide lawns and winding walks.

GARDEN D3
There were trees and flowerbeds.

GARDEN D4
There was a pool with a fountain in the middle.

GARDEN D5
But the flowerbeds were bare and the fountain was dry.

GARDEN /BEN
There was a vegetable garden too, and a gardener in it.

> *BEN, a cranky old gardener, picks up his hoe. The music ends. The other Garden actors move upstage.*

BEN
Every time the wind blows from the East my old bones growl and grumble. And every day I get achier and achier. But every day I'm here, working away, and nobody cares. It's enough to make you sick.

GARDEN /ROBIN
There were birds in the garden, too.

> *ROBIN, a full size actor who sings all lines, picks up the bird puppet and gestures with it.*

Music 04: Robin Song A (Same arrangement for Robin Songs A, B, C)
Tune: Bridge from English Country Garden (Traditional)
Solo lines interspersed with underscoring

ROBIN
(singing, as always)
Worms! Yes, I want some worms!

BEN
(over the music)
Oh it's you. Where have you been, you cheeky little beggar?

ROBIN
How I'd love some tasty worms!

BEN
(over the music)
You always come see what I'm doing. You're the head gardener, you are.

ROBIN
Dig up worms, tasty worms!
I'd love some tasty worms
Dig up lots of tasty worms!

BEN
No worms today! The ground's too hard to dig.

Mary enters.

MARY
(rudely)
Who are you?

BEN
You can call me Ben.

MARY
Why is the garden all brown?

BEN
Nothing grows in winter. Don't you know that?

Music 05: Robin Song B (Same arrangement for Robin Songs A, B, C)

ROBIN
Who is that? A little girl!

MARY
(over the music, enchanted by Robin)
Oh! What is that?

BEN
A robin—the friendliest bird there is.

ROBIN
Who is that? Come be my friend!

MARY
(over the music)
Oh! Do you think he likes me?

BEN
Yes, he wants to make friends.

ROBIN
Come with me, let's be friends!
I'd like to have more friends!
We'll be friends inside my garden!

> *Robin joins the Garden group.*

MARY
He's flown behind that wall! I want to follow him! There must be a door somewhere.

BEN
None as anyone can find, and none as is anyone's business. And especially not yours.

> *Ben puts his hoe in the box and*
> *joins the Garden group.*

MARY
I wish I could follow the robin. Maybe he'll come back.

GARDEN/DICKON
There was a cheerful whistle, and a boy came into view.

> *DICKON, a friendly local lad,*
> *puts on a jacket with a squirrel*
> *on the shoulder.*

MARY
Oh, look at the little animal!

DICKON
This is my squirrel Nutshell. Are you the girl from India?

MARY
Yes. Who are you?

DICKON
I'm Dickon. I came to visit my sister Martha.

MARY
Oh, her. I don't like her.

DICKON
Not like Martha! How can that be?

MARY
But I do like Nutshell. And I'm friends with a robin who was just here.

DICKON
Oh, I'm friends with him too. Watch this.

Dickon whistles and Robin comes forward.

Music 06: Robin Song C (Same arrangement for Robin Songs A, B, C)

ROBIN
Oh hello! It's you again!

MARY
(over the music)
Will he always come when you call?

DICKON
Yes. I've known him since he was hatched.

ROBIN
Oh hello! Now look at me!

DICKON
(over the music)
Yes, you are a fine fellow, aren't you?

MARY
He's the finest bird ever!

ROBIN
She is right, don't you know,
I am the finest bird!
She is right, I am the finest!

MARY
I do like you, Robin!

THE SECRET GARDEN

SFX: The clock chimes twelve.

DICKON
It's time for your noon meal.

MARY
Will I see you again?

DICKON
I'm here most days.

MARY
Oh. Um, goodbye then.

> *Mary exits. Dickon puts his costume in the box and joins the Garden group as they come forward.*

GARDEN E1
The robin gave a little shake of his wings and flew away.

GARDEN E2
He had other things to do.

GARDEN E3
He had other songs to sing.

GARDEN E4
He came into our garden—the secret garden.

GARDEN E5
He was the only bright thing among all the dead flowers.

Music 07: Robin in the Garden
Tune: English Country Garden (Traditional)
Vocal chorus

GARDEN
How many songbirds fly to and fro
In our lonely secret garden?

ROBIN
If there is one who's finer than me,
I will surely beg your pardon.

GARDEN
Listen, there's a nightingale!

ROBIN
Sounds just like a sickly whale.

GARDEN
She is not as fine a bird!

ROBIN
Right!

GARDEN
Other birds are dull and gray,

ROBIN
I'll outshine them any day.

GARDEN
You're the finest bird we've heard!

ROBIN
I know!

GARDEN
There is joy in the Spring

ADD ROBIN
**When Robin starts to sing
In our lonely secret garden.**

*Mary enters, running, into the
main garden. Robin gets the key
from the box.*

MARY
Robin! Oh Robin! Won't you come out?

GARDEN F1
The robin fluttered down next to the path where Mary was walking.

GARDEN F2
He hopped about under some bushes.

GARDEN F3
He stopped to look for a worm...

THE SECRET GARDEN

GARDEN F4
...Right next to a new molehill.

GARDEN F5
There was a ring of rusty iron in the earth.

ALL GARDEN
It was a key!

Robin drops the key and runs off to the Garden group. Mary picks up the key.

MARY
Perhaps it is the key to the garden! If only I could find the door!

Music 08: Lost and Forgotten Reprise A Shortened Vocal Chorus

ALL GARDEN
Lost and forgotten,
Waiting for Spring.
Here in the garden we sorrow and sing.
Here in the garden we sorrow and sing!

GARDEN G1
The next day, Mary wanted to look for the door...

GARDEN G2
But it rained.

GARDEN G3
And rained.

GARDEN G4
And rained.

GARDEN G5
Mary had to stay inside the manor.

Mary puts the key in her pocket and sulks inside the house. Mrs. Medlock joins her.

MARY
I want to go out! I want to go out!

MRS. MEDLOCK
Well, you can't. Go find a book to read!

GARDEN/COLIN
Aaaaaaaaaaaaaaaah!

MARY
There's that crying again.

MRS. MEDLOCK
Pay no attention. It's the wind.

MARY
I'll go exploring in some of the empty rooms.

> *Mary wanders to another part of the stage.*

GARDEN/COLIN
Wherever she went in the house, she heard the strange crying.

> *COLIN gets in the wheelchair (if he wasn't there already). Martha wheels him forward to meet Mary.*

COLIN
Aaaaaaaaaaaaaaaah!

MARY
Oh! Who are you?

COLIN
Go away, don't look at me!

MARY
You can't tell me what to do!

MARTHA
Actually, he can, Miss Mary. This is your cousin Colin. Master Colin, this is your cousin Mary from India.

COLIN
I don't want her. *(to Mary)* Go away!

MARY
Fine.

Mary starts to exit.

COLIN
No wait! Stay here and tell me all about India. Now!

MARY
I won't.

MARTHA
Now, Master Colin, if you're not polite, Miss Mary won't want to stay with you.

Music : 11 I Don't Care B
Vocal Chorus

COLIN
I don't care! I don't care!
If people don't like me.
I know that I'm grouchy, unhappy and slouchy,
As sulky as can be.

COLIN, MARY, MARTHA
I don't care! I don't care! (He won't care)
If I do (he does) get that mean and stony stare,
No one can amaze me (him),
Dislike cannot daze me (him)

COLIN
'Cause I don't care!

COLIN
(to Mary)
You! Tell me about India! Stay here!

MARY
I'll sit and clench my teeth and never tell you one thing.

Mary and Colin glare at each other.

COLIN
You are a selfish thing!

MARY
You're the most selfish boy I ever saw!

COLIN
You're stubborn!

MARY
So are you!

Mary and Colin glare at each other some more. Suddenly they start to laugh.

COLIN
You may go, Martha. My cousin and I will be fine.

MARTHA
Are you sure?

COLIN
Go! Go now, or I'll start screaming!

Martha joins the Garden group.

MARY
Do you ever go outside?

COLIN
No, I don't like people looking at me.

MARY
What's wrong with you anyway?

COLIN
I'm very weak. They say I may die, just like my mother did.

MARY
Your mother! Why, it's her garden I've been looking for.

COLIN
You have? Take me there at once!

MARY
I have the key, but I haven't found the door.

COLIN
I will help you find it. We just need a strong boy to push my chair.

MARY
We'll ask Dickon! He's Martha's brother.

COLIN
Very well. Martha! Martha!

THE SECRET GARDEN

Martha comes to push Colin across the stage, with Mary following. They meet with Dickon, who takes over pushing the chair.

GARDEN H1
The next clear day, they set out to find the garden.

GARDEN H2
All the walls of the garden were covered with ivy.

GARDEN H3
They looked and looked, but couldn't find the door.

GARDEN H4
Dickon and Colin investigated the west wall.

GARDEN H5
Mary looked at the south wall.

Dickon and Colin go to one side of the stage, Mary comes downstage center.

MARY
I wish I could see under all this ivy!

Robin seems to point at the wall. A Garden actor takes a doorknob from the box.

ROBIN
(singing a capella)
Look here! Look here! I found the door!

Mary looks closely at the wall., searching where Robin has pointed.

Music 12: Lost and Forgotten Reprise B
Lines interspersed with underscoring

ALL GARDEN
Lost and forgotten...

MARY
(over the music)
The wind blew the ivy away. Oh! Oh! A keyhole!

ALL GARDEN
Lost and forgotten…

> *Mary takes the key from her pocket and unlocks the door. The actor holding the doorknob swings in like a door. Mary enters as the Garden sings.*

ALL GARDEN
Oh, how we'll listen when somebody calls.

MARY
It's lovely, but so sad and brown! Dickon! Colin!

> *Mary goes to the door and calls out. Dickon and Colin hurry over to join her.*

ROBIN
(singing a capella)
Over here! I found the door!

MARY
Look!

> *Dickon and Colin enter the garden area and look around in wonder.*

COLIN
My mother's garden!

DICKON
I've heard of this place, but never really believed in it.

MARY
(to Dickon, anxiously)
Is it alive still? Or has everything died?

DICKON
Everything seems to be alive, just waiting for the Spring.

> **Music 11: Wait Till the Sun Shines A**
> **Tune: Wait Till the Sun Shines, Nellie (Von Tilzer and Sterling, 1905)**
> **Vocal chorus**

DICKON
Wait till the sun shines, Mary
When the clouds go drifting by!

GARDEN
We will start blooming, Mary,
Don't you sigh!

DICKON
Here in the secret garden,
Spring is drawing nigh,

DICKON & GARDEN (NO MARY, COLIN)
Wait till the sun shines,
Sparkling in the sky!

COLIN
Can't we help make things grow?

DICKON
Sure, if we just do a little weeding and pruning.

COLIN
We'll start today. Now!

Mary and Dickon get some gardening tools from the box. They get down on their knees and start weeding. Colin supervises. The Robin helps.

COLIN
There's big weed over here.

DICKON
I'll get it.

ROBIN
(singing a capella)
Over here! I found a worm!

DICKON
Now, don't take too many. Worms are good for a garden.

MARY
Are they? I didn't know that.

> *During the following song, the Garden actors become more and more colorful, adding scarves and other costume pieces (or removing their gray/brown outer clothes) to show how the flowers are blooming.*

Music 12: Old-Fashioned Garden
Tune: An Old-Fashioned Garden (Cole Porter, 1919)
Vocal verse, Vocal Chorus

ROBIN
Through all the years and all the tears
How the garden was filled with such strife,
Then came the girl, leaves started to unfurl
Till the garden was bursting with life;

GARDEN GROUP OR SOLO
There were the phlox,

GARDEN GROUP OR SOLO
Tall hollyhocks,

GARDEN GROUP OR SOLO
Violets perfuming the air,

GARDEN GROUP OR SOLO
Frail eglantines,

GARDEN GROUP OR SOLO
Shy columbines,

ALL GARDEN
And daffodils everywhere!

ALL GARDEN , ROBIN
It was an old-fashioned garden
Just an old-fashioned garden
But it carried us on
To a dream that was gone
In the land of long ago.
There was an old-fashioned bower
Filled with old-fashioned flowers

**In that old-fashioned garden
Where the sweet roses grow.**

COLIN
I want to stay here forever and ever!

Ben appears at the garden door.

BEN
Here, what's this? You kids don't belong in here. Shoo!

COLIN
Do you know who I am? This is <u>my</u> garden. It belonged to my mother.

BEN
You! But everyone always says that the Craven boy is sickly and can't move a muscle!

COLIN
How dare they talk about me like that? I'm not sickly!

BEN
Then why are you in that chair?

COLIN
I'll show you, old man!

Colin struggles to his feet, with Mary and Dickon helping.

COLIN
You see? I'm not weak! I'm strong here in this garden!

BEN
Well lad, I guess I was wrong. And you do look like your mother, now that I notice.

MARY
Did you know Colin's mother?

BEN
Oh yes, I spent many an hour in here helping with her roses.

ROBIN
(singing a capella)
Roses are blooming now!

COLIN
Come help us!

> *Ben starts hoeing. Colin walks slowly around and around, gathering confidence all the while.*

GARDEN I1
Summer came, and every day, Colin walked a little farther.

GARDEN I2
Every day, more flowers bloomed.

GARDEN I3
Every day, Mary was happier and happier.

GARDEN I4
There was only one sad person left.

GARDEN I5
Poor Mr. Craven still thought his son was weak and sickly.

> *Mr. Craven gets his cane and meets up with Mrs. Medlock.*

MR. CRAVEN
I'm back, Mrs. Medlock.

MRS. MEDLOCK
Welcome home, sir.

MR. CRAVEN
How is Colin? Is he—better?

MRS. MEDLOCK
To tell the truth, sir, he might be better and he might be changing for the worse.

> *Martha joins them*

MARTHA
He goes outdoors every day with Miss Mary!

MRS. MEDLOCK
He used to eat nothing and then suddenly he began to eat something enormous!

MARTHA
He laughs all the time instead of screaming!

MR. CRAVEN
I should go see him, then. Come with me.

They cross slowly to the garden.

GARDEN J1
In the garden, there was light and sunshine.

GARDEN J2
In the garden, there were children laughing.

GARDEN J3
In the garden, there were birds singing.

GARDEN J4
In the garden, there were flowers blooming

GARDEN J5
In the garden, there was a smiling girl and a healthy boy.

Colin grabs something from Mary and runs out the door. She and Dickon chase him, laughing. They stop short when they see Mr. Craven.

MR. CRAVEN
Who—What? Who?!?

COLIN
Father, it's me.

MR. CRAVEN
Colin?

COLIN
You can't believe it. I scarcely can myself.

MRS. MEDLOCK
How could this be?

MARTHA
Dickon! What's happening here?

MARY
It was the garden that did it—it's magic!

DICKON
The garden is magic, sir.

MR. CRAVEN
It was your mother's garden. Now it's yours.

COLIN
Aren't you glad, Father? I'm going to live forever and ever and ever!

MR. CRAVEN
Take me into the garden, my boy. And tell me all about it.

They all enter the garden. Everyone has colorful clothes and wraps. The back curtain opens, revealing a wall of color and light.

Music 13: Wait Till the Sun Shines B (Finale)
Vocal Chorus, Underscoring, Vocal Chorus

COLIN
Here's where the sun shines, Father
When the clouds go drifting by.

MARY
We will be happy, Uncle,
Don't you sigh!

DICKON
Here in the secret garden,
Summertime is high,

COLIN
Here's where the sun shines,
Sparkling in the sky!

GARDEN K1
(over the music)
This was the story of a garden...

GARDEN K2
A garden that died...

GARDEN K3
And came back to life again.

GARDEN K4
It was also the story of the girl who learned to love the garden.

GARDEN K5
And to love other people as well.

> *Mr. Craven draws Colin to his side, then Mary. They form a family group while the other names characters gather around them. The Garden actors form as big a semicircle as needed. They all sing.*

COLIN
Here's where the sun shines, Father
When the clouds go drifting by.

MARY
We will be happy, Uncle,
Don't you sigh!

MR. CRAVEN
Here in the secret garden,
Summertime is high,

ALL
Here's where the sun shines,
Sparkling in the sky!

THE END

ROBIN HOOD AND THE MERRY BAND

CHARACTERS (in order of appearance)

Robin Hood	M/F	Outlaw, leader of the Merry Band
Little John	M	Large outlaw, Robin's friend
Friar Tuck	M	Monk outlaw, fierce fighter
Scarlett	F	Outlaw, dressed in red
Alan-a Dale	M/F	Outlaw, minstrel, carries/plays ukulele and recorder
Much	M/F	Peasant who becomes an outlaw
Hawk	M/F	Peasant who becomes an outlaw
Lady/Maid Marian	F	Lady of the court, niece of Prince John
Gwendolyn	F	Marian's sweet attendant
Griselda	F	Marian's grumpy attendant
Captain Gisborne	M/F	Leader of the guards
Guards	2 M/F	Number open (at least two)
Prince John	M	Greedy, lazy ruler
Jujubee	M/F	Court Jester
Sheriff	M	Tax collector, villainous

4 M, 4 F, 8 M or F

16 plus additional outlaws, guards or ladies as desired

STRUCTURE

Scene 1: Sherwood Forest (Songs: *Our Merry Band, Lunch on the Green, The Noble Princely John, Sheriff's Song, We Know Where We're Going*)

Interlude: Various locations in the castle (No songs)

Scene 2: The Fairgrounds (Songs: *Dancing So Long at the Fair, Our Merry Band*)

LENGTH

30-40 minutes

NOTE

The original production used bows but no arrows. We had a length of elastic running between the bowstring and wood. This looked like an arrow as the string was pulled back. An arrow sound effect completed the illusion.

Scene 1: Sherwood Forest

A few trees and maybe a log to sit on. ROBIN HOOD, LITTLE JOHN, FRIAR TUCK, SCARLETT, ALAN-A DALE and other members of the original Merry Band are discovered onstage.

Music 01: Our Merry Band
Tune: Come, Lasses and Lads (English folk song)
Vocal chorus, instrumental interlude, vocal half-chorus

OUTLAWS, ROBIN
Come, lasses and lads,
Take leave of your dads
And off to the forest flee.
In Sherwood fair you'll find us there
For an outlaw band are we.

ROBIN
We take from the rich and sleek
And give to the poor and meek.

OUTLAWS, ROBIN
When Robin lets his/her arrows fly,
The villains all run and cry.
Our Merry Band is taking a stand,
For justice throughout the land.

Interlude: The Merry Band carouses to the music. Alan-a Dale "plays" a recorder.

ROBIN
We take from the rich and sleek
And give to the poor and meek.

OUTLAWS, ROBIN
When Robin lets his/her arrows fly,
The villains all run and cry.
Our Merry Band is taking a stand,
For justice throughout the land.

> *The Merry Band ends the song in a characteristically heroic but jolly pose.*

ROBIN
What ho, Friar Tuck, how is our stock of food?

FRIAR TUCK
There's plenty to share with the village, if Little John doesn't slop it all over himself.

LITTLE JOHN
Who're you calling sloppy?

FRIAR TUCK
You, ya big slob!

LITTLE JOHN
Oh yeah?

FRIAR TUCK
Yeah!

> *Little John and Friar Tuck face off like they're going to fight.*

ROBIN
Cut it out! Don't you two ever get tired of arguing?

> *Little John and Friar Tuck break apart. Little John throws his arm around Friar Tuck's shoulders. Friar Tuck shrugs him off.*

LITTLE JOHN
Naw, we like fighting, don't we Friar?

FRIAR TUCK
Yeah, but I'd rather fight with the Sheriff's tax collectors.

ROBIN
Me too!

OUTLAWS
Us too!

ALAN-A
Ahem!

Every time Alan-a says "Ahem," he/she plays a random chord on the ukulele, and sings off-key)

ALAN-A
(continued, singing)
Hey nonny nonny, fa la la,
The Sheriff has a fatal flaw
He gets rich and soft by taxing the poor,
Till the Merry Band shows his guards what-for.

OUTLAWS
Ugh!

The outlaws groan. Alan-a pays no attention.

ALAN-A
That's the song for us, isn't it, Scarlett?

SCARLETT
Fiddle-dee-dee! It's the right idea, but your singing is terrible!

ROBIN
C'mon, Scarlett, we all pretend we like it. It's a Merry Band tradition, right everybody?

OUTLAWS
Right!

LITTLE JOHN
(looking offstage)
Quiet, I hear something!

FRIAR TUCK
(looking offstage in the same direction)
Here come two outsiders!

ROBIN
Hide, but be ready to fight, everybody!

The outlaws "hide" or go just offstage. Robin waits alone.

*MUCH and HAWK enter.
(Hawk can be omitted, if necessary.)*

ROBIN
Halt, strangers! What brings you to Sherwood?

MUCH
We're looking for the Merry Band of outlaws.

HAWK
Yeah, are you them?

ROBIN
Why do you seek the Merry Band?

MUCH
The Sheriff of Nottingham just collected taxes from the village.

HAWK
Yeah, he called them "taxes."

ROBIN
He may say they're taxes, but he gives a little to Prince John and keeps the rest for himself!

The outlaws creep forward to listen.

LITTLE JOHN
The Sheriff is a thief!

FRIAR TUCK
He steals from the poor!

SCARLETT
And makes himself rich!

OUTLAWS
Down with the Sheriff! Boo!

LITTLE JOHN
The same thing happened to us!

FRIAR TUCK
That's why we're here!

SCARLETT
We've all lost everything!

MUCH
I was so proud of my chickens!

HAWK
The Sheriff even took the eggs!

ALAN-A
Ahem!
Hey nonny nonny, poor sad Much
Fell into the Sheriff's clutch!
Lost the farm and chickens and such
Because the tax was way too much!

OUTLAWS
Ugh!

ALAN-A
Get it? Too <u>much</u> tax. Too <u>much</u> for <u>Much</u>!

SCARLETT
We got it. We just didn't think it was funny.

ROBIN
What ho, Merry Band! What shall we do about Much and Hawk?

LITTLE JOHN
I'd say the Merry Band just got bigger.

FRIAR TUCK
The more the merrier, I always say!

OUTLAWS
Huzzah!

The outlaws greet Much and
Hawk with handshakes, pats
on the back, etc.

OUTLAWS
(ad lib)
Welcome! Here's to new members! We're glad you're here!

ROBIN
Let's take our new members with us as we give our extra food to the villagers!

OUTLAW GROUP 1
Take from the rich!

OUTLAW GROUP 2
Give to the poor!

ROBIN
Follow me, Merry Band!

> *The Merry Band exits.*
>
> *MARIAN, GWENDOLYN and GRISELDA (plus any added LADIES) enter from the other direction, carrying at least one picnic basket. CAPTAIN Gisborne follows them.*

MARIAN
What do you think, Gwendolyn? Is this a good spot for a picnic?

GWENDOLYN
It looks good to me, Lady Marian. What do you think, Griselda?

GRISELDA
Humph! I suppose it will have to do.

CAPTAIN
I don't like it. These woods are full of dangerous outlaws.

LADIES
Eek! Outlaws!

> *Every time they say "Eek!" the Ladies cling together and look around as though the outlaws will drop out of the trees.*

MARIAN
I'm not afraid of outlaws. They're just village people who've been driven out of their homes.

GWENDOLYN
They'll take all our jewels!

GRISELDA
They'll kidnap us for ransom!

LADIES
Eek! Outlaws!

CAPTAIN
Lady Marian, I'm not sure I can protect you by myself.

MARIAN
We'll be fine, Captain Gisborne. Go keep watch if you're so nervous.

CAPTAIN
Very well, I'll be right over here.

Captain Gisborne exits.

GWENDOLYN
Lady Marian, are you sure it's safe out here?

GRISELDA
There could be outlaws behind every bush!

LADIES
Eek! Outlaws!

MARIAN
Oh, let's not worry so much when it's such a lovely day for a picnic.

Music 02: Lunch on the Green
Tune: Lavender's Blue (English folk song)
Vocal chorus

MARIAN
Lunch in the woods,
Pretty ladies

LADIES
Lunch on the green!

MARIAN
We'll have a feast,
Pretty ladies

MARIAN, LADIES
Fit for a queen!

They look through the items in their basket.

MARIAN
Chicken and cheese,
Pretty ladies

LADIES
Peaches and cream!

MARIAN
We'll have a feast,
Pretty ladies

MARIAN, LADIES
Out of a dream!
We'll feast like a queen,
With lunch on the green!

Captain Gisborne enters. The Ladies move the basket out of the way for the next song.

CAPTAIN
(announcing)
His Royal Highness, Prince John!

PRINCE John enters, waving.

PRINCE
Greetings, greetings, blah blah blah. *(yawning)* Ah Marian, there you are.

JUJUBEE
(offstage)
Hey! Announce me, too!

CAPTAIN
Oh yes, and the Court Jester, Jujubee.

JUJUBEE bounds onstage.

JUJUBEE
Here I am! Now ye olde party can starteth! Forsooth, nonny nonny and woo-hoo!

MARIAN
(to the Prince)
What are you doing here, Uncle?

PRINCE
I was worried about you being out here in the woods, Marian. *(yawning)* After all, you are my favorite niece.

JUJUBEE
Of course, you are his <u>only</u> niece. Woo-hoo!

PRINCE
(yawning)
There is that.

MARIAN
And what exactly are you and the Court Jester going to do to protect me?

PRINCE
Oh, we're not alone. *(calling offstage)* Guards!

> *The GUARDS (at least two)*
> *enter and stand at attention.*

GUARDS
Here we are! Ready for duty!

CAPTAIN
At ease, guards!

GUARDS
Like this? *(scrambling around)* Or like this?

CAPTAIN
Quiet! Act like guards, for once!

JUJUBEE
You're supposed to be so splendid! Woo-hoo!

Music 03: The Noble Princely John
Tune: The Grand Old Duke of York (English folk song)
Two vocal choruses

JUJUBEE
Oh, the noble, princely John

PRINCE
(yawning)
That's me!

JUJUBEE
He had such splendid guards!

CAPTAIN, GUARDS
That's us!

> *The Guards and Captain march around. Prince John yawns.*

JUJUBEE
He marched them forward to the top of a hill
Then he marched them all backwards!

CAPTAIN, GUARDS
That's hard!

JUJUBEE, MARIAN, LADIES
And when they were up,
They were up.

CAPTAIN, GUARDS
Like this!

JUJUBEE, MARIAN, LADIES
And when they were down,
They were down.

CAPTAIN, GUARDS
Like that!

ALL EXCEPT PRINCE
And when they (we) were only halfway up,
They (we) were neither up nor down.

PRINCE
I'm the noble, princely John

JUJUBEE
That's him!

PRINCE
(yawning)
Ah-ah-ah-ah-ah-ah!

JUJUBEE, CAPTAIN, GUARDS
What's that?

> *Jujubee joins the marching, throwing the Guards and Captain into even more confusion.*

PRINCE
**I marched them backward to the top of a hill
Then I marched them all forwards!**

JUJUBEE, CAPTAIN, GUARDS
How's that?

MARIAN, LADIES
**And when they were down,
They were down.**

JUJUBEE, CAPTAIN, GUARDS
Like this?

MARIAN, LADIES
**And when they were up,
They were up.**

JUJUBEE, CAPTAIN, GUARDS
Like that?

ALL
**And when they (we) were only halfway down,
They (we) were neither down nor up.**

GUARDS
What?

> *Jujubee, the Guards and Captain end up in a confused heap. The Captain tries to get the Guards back in order.*

CAPTAIN
Line up! Attention! C'mon, people, shape up!

GUARDS
Like this? *(scrambling around)* Or like this?

CAPTAIN
Quiet! Show the Prince some respect!

PRINCE
(yawning)
That's enough excitement for now!

JUJUBEE
More excitement than he's used to! Woo-hoo!

PRINCE
(yawning)
Oh Marian, I almost forgot. I brought along your favorite person.

LADIES
Ooh, who could it be?

JUJUBEE
He means me, of course! Woo-hoo!

PRINCE
No, I mean—

> *The Sheriff enters, wearing gold chains, bracelets and rings.*

SHERIFF
(posing)
Me! The great, talented and handsome Sheriff of Nottingham!

MARIAN
Actually, I'd rather see the Jester.

SHERIFF
My dear Lady Marian, you know we belong together!

MARIAN
I most certainly do not know that!

PRINCE
(yawning)
Well, I guess we'll let you two talk it over. Come, Captain!

CAPTAIN
Yes, your highness.

> *The Prince and Captain exit.*

JUJUBEE
Hey! How can you go away without me to entertain you? Woo-hoo!

Jujubee runs after the Prince and Captain.

SHERIFF
Now, Lady Marian, let us enjoy a sweet picnic in the woods— *(looking at the Ladies)* alone.

GWENDOLYN
Oh! Do you mean us?

GRISELDA
Humph! We can take a hint.

The Ladies start to leave.

MARIAN
No! I'd like to have my friends here.

The Ladies come back.

SHERIFF
We need to have a private talk. Go, ladies!

The Ladies start to leave.

MARIAN
No! Stay here, ladies.

The Ladies come back.

SHERIFF
Now, Lady Marian, let us be reasonable…

MARIAN
I'm telling you, Sheriff, if they go, I go.

SHERIFF
Fine. The ladies can stay.

The Ladies sit down.

GWENDOLYN
Whew! I was getting dizzy!

GRISELDA
Humph! About time they made up their minds.

MARIAN
All right, Sheriff. What do you want, anyway?

SHERIFF
I want you to be my partner!

MARIAN
Partner? Why?

SHERIFF
The village people trust you. They'll tell you where they've hidden their valuables, and then you can tell me, and then I'll double the taxes I collect, and then we'll both get rich, rich, rich!

MARIAN
No, no, no! I would never do anything so underhanded!

SHERIFF
But it's lots of fun! Everyone bows before me and my extreme cleverness!

Music 04: Sheriff's Song
Tune: The Sheriff of Nottingham (from "Robin Hood" by deKoven, 1891)
Vocal chorus

SHERIFF
I am the Sheriff of Nottingham!
My eye is like the eagle's.
So sly and clever, in fact I am
A genius quite

GUARDS
Such a wonderful sight!

SHERIFF
I'm considered remarkably bright!

GUARDS, LADIES
You're so bright!

SHERIFF
If anyone fractures the lightest law,

GUARDS
(to the Ladies)
Bow low, bow low!

> *The Ladies curtsy. Marian does not.*

SHERIFF
A glance from my eye
Fills their mind with awe.

GUARDS
(to the Ladies)
Bow lower still, bow low!
Bow low!

SHERIFF
(to the Ladies)
I would if I were you!

> *The Ladies curtsy so low that they nearly fall over. Marian watches..*

SHERIFF, GUARDS, LADIES
You may seek days three
But you never will see
Such a wondrous Sheriff as me (he)!
Such a wondrous Sheriff as me, me, me! (he, he, he)!

SHERIFF
The Sheriff of Nottingham!

GUARDS
(to the Ladies)
Bow!

> *The Ladies fall to the ground.*

LADIES
(ad lib)
Oh dear! Humph! That was embarrassing!

SHERIFF
You see, dear lady, I am a person who can be helpful to you.

MARIAN
I don't want your kind of "help," Sheriff.

> *The Merry Band makes some offstage noise.*

SHERIFF
What's that?

GUARDS
(ad lib, looking in different directions)
Who's there? Someone's sneaking up on us! Watch out!

SHERIFF
It's probably that dratted Robin Hood and those terrible outlaws.

LADIES
Eek! Outlaws!

ROBIN
(offstage)
Go to it, Merry Band!

OUTLAW GROUP 1
(leaping onstage)
Take from the rich!

OUTLAW GROUP 2
(leaping onstage)
Give to the poor!

> *The Merry Band attacks. They chase the Guards off one way and the Ladies off the other. A Lady picks up the picnic basket as she runs off. Little John grabs the Sheriff by the arms and Scarlett grabs Marian.*

GUARDS
(ad lib during the attack)
Oh no! They're after us! They're scary! Let's run for it!

LADIES
(ad lib during the attack)
Eek! Outlaws! They'll take our picnic! Let's run for it!

OUTLAWS
(ad lib during the attack)
Now we've got you! Come now, we won't hurt you! We just want your gold! You can run, but you can't hide!

At the end of the tussle, the only people onstage are Little John with the Sheriff on one side, Scarlett with Marian on the other, and Robin in the middle.

NOTE: It's important that the Sheriff never gets to see Robin. Robin and the other outlaws should stay upstage, while Little John keeps the Sheriff facing the audience. Scarlett does the same with Marian. The Sheriff keeps struggling to get free or turn around, while Marian stands quietly.

ROBIN
(to Marian)
Welcome to Sherwood, my lady! We're honored to have you with us!

SHERIFF
Go away, we don't speak to outlaws.

ROBIN
I wasn't talking to you.

SHERIFF
Don't you know who I am?

LITTLE JOHN
Oh, we know who you are, Sheriff.

The other Outlaws return, carrying the guards' weapons and the picnic basket.

FRIAR TUCK
And we're not impressed, Sheriff.

ALAN-A
Ahem!
Hey nonny nonny, tee hee hee,
The Sheriff's caught, we all agree
Without his guards, he's not so bold
He sure does have a lot of gold!

SCARLETT
He is wearing an awful lot of gold!

MUCH
I bet it came from our taxes!

HAWK
Yeah, what Much said!

ROBIN
I think we should put that gold to better use!

OUTLAW GROUP 1
Take from the rich!

OUTLAW GROUP 2
Give to the poor!

The Outlaws grab the Sheriff's gold chains, bracelets and rings.

SHERIFF
You'll be sorry for this!

ROBIN
The people in the village won't be sorry when they get to eat tonight. Now, go!

SHERIFF
And leave all my precious gold here? Never!

ROBIN
Go, or we'll take your clothes too!

OUTLAWS
(ad lib)
You'll look funny going back to the castle in your underwear! Get out of here! Nyah nyah nyah!

SHERIFF
Curse you, Robin Hood! I'll get my revenge if it's the last thing I do!

The Sheriff runs off. The Outlaws follow for a few steps, then come back.

MARIAN
And what about me? Take my gold too.

Marian holds out her bracelet. Robin takes it, surprised.

ROBIN
Why thank you, my lady.

MUCH
Hey, I know her! She brought soup to my family when we were sick!

HAWK
Yeah, me too!

ROBIN
You can let her go, Scarlett.

Scarlett releases Marian, who
turns quietly to face Robin.

MARIAN
Yes, I'm on your side. I've come to Sherwood to find Robin Hood and the Merry Band.

OUTLAWS
That's us.

ROBIN
What does a lady from the court want with us?

MARIAN
I want to help you, even if I get in trouble with the Prince and the Sheriff.

ROBIN
Are you sure? We are on a very special mission, aren't we, Merry Band?

OUTLAWS
Yes!

Music 05: We Know Where We're Going
Tunes: I Know Where I'm Going and Country Garden (Scottish and English Folk Songs)
Vocal chorus, bridge from Country Garden, Vocal half-chorus

ROBIN
We know where we're going,
And we know who's going with us,

OUTLAWS
Right!

ROBIN
I'm proud to be the leader
Of the Merry Band of Sherwood!

MARIAN
I know what I want,
And who I want to follow,
Let me be a member
Of the Merry Band of Sherwood!

OUTLAW GROUP 1
We all sleep out in the rain,

OUTLAW GROUP 2
Cold and wet and full of pain,

ALL OUTLAWS
It's no life for such a lady!

OUTLAW GROUP 1
Eating only what we can,

OUTLAW GROUP 2
Burnt and lumpy from the pan

ALL OUTLAWS
It's not right for such a lady!

ROBIN, OUTLAWS
We know where we're going,
And we know who's going with us,

ROBIN
I'm proud to be the leader
Of the Merry Band of Sherwood!

ROBIN, OUTLAWS
The Merry Band of Sherwood!

ROBIN
Why would we want you in our band, anyway?

LITTLE JOHN
Yeah, why? What can you do for us?

MARIAN
I'm very good with a bow and arrow.

FRIAR TUCK
Ha! You're talking to the best archer in England.

ROBIN
(pointing offstage)
So, my lady, could you shoot that acorn over there?

MARIAN
(pointing to a closer spot)
You mean that brown one in the nearest tree?

> *Robin aims his/her bow offstage.*

ROBIN
No, the green one hanging right… over… there…

> *Robin shoots an arrow offstage.*

SFX: Arrow whizzing and hitting a target

OUTLAWS
(ad lib)
Wow! Bullseye! Clean as a whistle! Huzzah, Robin!

MARIAN
That's amazing. I can't shoot like that.

ROBIN
I'd say, don't come back until you can. But thanks for the offer.

MARIAN
Oh well. I guess I'll just go back to the castle.

> *Marian exits sadly.*

FRIAR TUCK
Too bad. She sure wanted to join us.

SCARLETT
That wasn't really fair.

ALAN-A
Yeah, none of us can shoot as well as Robin either.

LITTLE JOHN
But she's too fine a lady for the likes of us.

ROBIN
We are happy the way we are. Right, Merry Band?

OUTLAWS
Right!

> **Music 06: Reprise: We Know Where We're Going**
> **Vocal half- chorus**

ROBIN, OUTLAWS
We know where we're going,
And we know who's going with us,

ROBIN
I'm proud to be the leader
Of the Merry Band of Sherwood!

ROBIN, OUTLAWS
The Merry Band of Sherwood!

The curtain closes.

END OF SCENE 1

Interlude: In front of the curtain

A bare stage. Jujubee enters carrying a gigantic scroll.

JUJUBEE
(reading the scroll)
Hear ye, hear ye! Prince John announces a grand fair to be held one month from today. There will be feasting, dancing and an archery contest.
(looking up from the scroll)
They forgot to mention my stand-up comic routine, but I'll be there too! Woo-hoo!

Jujubee does a little dance, then exits. The Prince and Sheriff enter and cross the stage as they talk.

SHERIFF
We need to think of a way to lure that dreadful Robin Hood to the fair…

PRINCE
(yawning)
Yes, yes, whatever you say.

SHERIFF
I know! We'll announce that whoever wins the archery contest will have no taxes on their village for a year.

PRINCE
(suddenly alert)
But that means I'd get less gold!

SHERIFF
Yes, but you'd have Robin Hood instead! Listen, I have a clever plan…

They exit. Jujubee enters and skips and prances across the stage.

JUJUBEE
One week till the fair! One week till the fair! Woo-hoo!

Jujubee exits. The Captain and Sheriff enter and cross the stage as they talk.

SHERIFF
Captain, I need you to arrest Robin Hood at the fair. That outlaw is sure to be at the archery contest.

CAPTAIN
But what if Robin Hood wears a disguise?

SHERIFF
That's no problem. You're the best archer in the guards, aren't you?

CAPTAIN
Well yes, I suppose I am.

SHERIFF
And Robin Hood is supposed to be the best archer in all of England?

CAPTAIN
So they say.

SHERIFF
Here's my plan: you'll shoot first, and then whoever beats you must be Robin Hood!

CAPTAIN
Oh, that's clever!

SHERIFF
All my plans are clever! That's because I'm so clever! Clever, clever, clever! Ha ha!

They exit. Jujubee enters, skipping.

JUJUBEE
Tomorrow, tomorrow, I love ya tomorrow! Then you may take me to the fair! Woo-hoo!

Jujubee does a little dance.

The curtain opens. Jujubee joins the other actors on stage.

END OF INTERLUDE

Scene 2: The Fairgrounds

A throne, audience seating, and space for an archery contest The Ladies and Guards (no Captain) are dancing. Jujubee joins them. At end of the instrumental, they all sing.

Music 07: Dancing So Long at the Fair, Part 1
Tune: Oh Dear, What Can the Matter Be (English Folk Song)
Instrumental intro, vocal chorus, instrumental interlude, vocal chorus

LADIES, GUARDS, JUJUBEE
Oh dear, where could my sweetheart be?
Oh dear, where could my sweetheart be?
Oh dear, where could my sweetheart be?
Dancing so long at the fair!

They dance to the instrumental music. Jujubee jumps and twirls.

LADIES, GUARDS, JUJUBEE
Oh dear, where could my sweetheart be?
Oh dear, where could my sweetheart be?
Oh dear, where could my sweetheart be?
Dancing so long at the fair!

PRINCE JOHN
(offstage)
Jujubee!

JUJUBEE
My master's voice! I must go spread joy elsewhere! Woo-hoo!

Jujubee does a little jump, then exits. The Ladies and Guards chat together.

The Merry Band (no Robin) enters.

LITTLE JOHN
I still think it's too dangerous for us to be here, especially for Robin.

FRIAR TUCK
Robin is safely disguised, so don't worry.

SCARLETT
And we're here to protect him/her.

ALAN-A
It's the only way to get our taxes back.

MUCH
And then I can have my chickens again!

HAWK
Yeah, what Much said!

LITTLE JOHN
Now that we're here, what do we do?

FRIAR TUCK
What do you think, silly?

LITTLE JOHN
Who're you calling silly?

FRIAR TUCK
You, ya big clown! Do what normal people do at a fair!

ALAN-A
Ahem!
Hey nonny nonny—

SCARLETT
(cutting Alan-a off)
No, that is <u>not</u> normal.

MUCH
I know! We should join the dancers!

HAWK
Yeah, what Much said!

OUTLAWS
Let's dance!

The Outlaws join the Ladies and Guards.

Music 08: Dancing So Long at the Fair, Part 2
Instrumental intro, vocal chorus, instrumental interlude, vocal chorus

LADIES, GUARDS, OUTLAWS
Oh dear, where could my sweetheart be?
Oh dear, where could my sweetheart be?
Oh dear, where could my sweetheart be?
Dancing so long at the fair!

They dance to the instrumental music. Alan-a plays along on the recorder.

LADIES, GUARDS, OUTLAWS
Oh dear, where could my sweetheart be?
Oh dear, where could my sweetheart be?
Oh dear, where could my sweetheart be?
Dancing so long at the fair!

The Captain enters with an archery bow.

CAPTAIN
Guards! Get back to your posts!

The Guards scramble to attention.

GUARDS
Like this? *(scrambling around)* Or like this?

CAPTAIN
(pointing offstage)
The rest of you, go get your free cider before the archery contest starts!

OUTLAWS
(ad lib, at the same time as the Ladies)
Cider! I have a tremendous thirst! Let me at it! Out of my way! Don't let this big slob drink it all!

LADIES
(ad lib, at the same time as the Outlaws)
All this dancing has made me thirsty! Humph! It's about time for the cider!

The Ladies and Outlaws exit.

CAPTAIN
(calling offstage in the other direction)
All clear, Sheriff!

The Sheriff enters.

SHERIFF
Ready for the contest, Captain?

CAPTAIN
(pointing offstage)
Yes, the target's over there.

SHERIFF
As soon as Robin Hood shoots, you arrest the scoundrel, no matter what the disguise may be. Get it?

CAPTAIN
Got it!

SHERIFF
Good!

CAPTAIN
Here comes the Prince!

SHERIFF
And that dratted Jujubee! I wish I could arrest him/her!

The Prince enters, followed by Jujubee, carrying the scroll.

PRINCE
(yawning)
All right, let's get this over with.

SHERIFF
Where's Lady Marian? I want her to see my triumph!

PRINCE
She's resting with a bad headache. *(yawning)* I wish I could take a nap.

JUJUBEE
(melodramatically)
Heavy lies the head that wears a crown!
(as usual)
Woo-hoo!

PRINCE
You've got that right. *(yawning)* Except for the woo-hoo part.

The Prince sits on his throne.
The Sheriff stands behind him.

CAPTAIN
Here come the fairgoers!

The Ladies and Outlaws enter
and sit in the audience area.

OUTLAWS
(ad lib, at the same time as the Ladies)
It's time for the contest! I'm ready to see some fancy shooting! That cider was delicious!

LADIES
(ad lib, at the same time as the Outlaws)
Ooh, I'm looking forward to the contest! Humph! It's about time the contest got started!

JUJUBEE
(reading the scroll)
Come one, come all and take your chance at the archery contest! Step right up and get this year's taxes canceled for your village! All you have to do is beat Captain Gisborne, the best archer in the guards!
(looking up from the scroll)
Woo-hoo!

An archer with a hood and
archery bow, disguised as a
peasant, enters. It is Robin, of
course. He/she pantomimes the
lines indicated in brackets.

ROBIN
(pantomiming)
[I want to be in the contest.]

CAPTAIN
What's that? What do you want?

ROBIN
(pantomiming)
[shoots an arrow]

LITTLE JOHN
It's Sibley the Silent!

FRIAR TUCK
He/she lives in our village.

MUCH
Such a shame, the poor thing can't talk.

HAWK
Yeah, what Much said!

ALAN-A
Ahem!
Sibley the Silent, fa la la la—

SCARLETT
(interrupting)
I wish you were Alan-a Silent.

ROBIN
(pantomiming)
[shoots another arrow]

SHERIFF
(quietly, to the Prince)
Silent, ha! I bet it's Robin Hood!

PRINCE
(yawning)
Oh, let the peasant shoot already.

> *The Captain gestures for Robin to come stand next to him.*

JUJUBEE
Anybody else want to try? It's fun! Woo-hoo!

> *Another disguised archer enters, in a full-length hooded cloak. It is Marian, with an archery bow.*

MARIAN
(in a low "masculine" voice)
I'd like to try my luck.

JUJUBEE
And what's your name, my good fellow?

MARIAN
(low "masculine" voice)
Er... Archibald the Archer.

SHERIFF
(quietly to the Prince)
Hmm, maybe <u>this</u> is Robin Hood and Sibley really <u>is</u> silent. That sure sounds like a false voice to me!

PRINCE
(yawning)
Yes, yes, maybe so. Get started, Captain!

CAPTAIN
Very well.
(to Guards)
Go stand on either side of the target.

GUARDS
(ad lib)
That sounds dangerous! What if you shoot us by mistake? I'm scared!

CAPTAIN
Do you really think I'll miss the target? You and you, go! Run!

> *Two of the Guards jog off to the target.*

CAPTAIN
(calling off)
After each shot, bring the target in for us to look at.

GUARDS
(offstage)
Will do!

JUJUBEE
Drum roll for the Captain, please! Brrrrrrrrr-woo-hoo!

> *The Captain aims and shoots.*

SFX: Arrow whizzing and hitting a target

ALL
(ad lib)
Looks like a bullseye! What a shot! The Captain is sure a great archer!

The offstage Guards enter with the target. There is an arrow dead center.

PRINCE JOHN
(yawning)
Well, that was a dull contest. Who can beat that?

SHERIFF
(quietly, to the Prince)
Let's see what Robin Hood will do…

CAPTAIN
Take the target back for Sibley's turn.

The Guards carry the target back offstage.

JUJUBEE
The crowd is hushed for the next shot—and so is Sibley the Silent! Woo-hoo!

Robin takes aim and shoots.

SFX: Arrow whizzing and hitting a target

The crowd stares in astonishment.

ALL
(ad lib)
Amazing! Sibley split the arrow!

The offstage Guards enter with the target. Now there are two arrows, with Robin's arrow splitting the Captain's.

SHERIFF
Only Robin Hood could do that!

CAPTAIN
Seize the archer disguised as Sibley!

The Guards surround Robin. The Outlaws prepare to attack.

MARIAN
(low "masculine" voice)
Hold! I have not had my chance!

CAPTAIN
What's the point?

PRINCE
(yawning)
Oh, let Archibald try!

SHERIFF
Sure, just try to beat that!

> *The Guards release Robin and carry the target back offstage.*

JUJUBEE
Now we'll find out why he's called Archibald the Archer-bald! Woo-hoo!

SCARLETT
(to Alan-a)
That sounds like one of your lines.

ALAN-A
Ooh! *(sings)* **Hey nonny—**

ALL
Sssshhhhhhhhhhhh!

> *Even Robin makes a "cut it out" gesture. Marian takes aim and shoots.*

SFX: Arrow whizzing and hitting a target

> *The crowd stares in even more astonishment.*

ALL
(ad lib)
Unbelievable! Look at that! Is it even possible?

> *The offstage Guards enter with the target. Now there are THREE arrows. Marian has split Robin's arrow.*

SHERIFF
Only Robin Hood could do <u>that</u>! And I mean it this time!

CAPTAIN
Seize the archer disguised as Archibald!

The Guards surround Marian.

MARIAN
(in her natural voice)
Think again! I am not Robin Hood!

Marian reveals her face.

ALL
(in astonishment)
Lady Marian!

JUJUBEE
She shoots, she scores! Woo-hoo!

MARIAN
I won the contest, so I claim a year free of tax for Sibley's village!

Robin pantomimes a cheer while the Outlaws shout.

OUTLAWS
Huzzah!

SHERIFF
(whimpering)
I don't understand. How could my clever plan go so wrong?

PRINCE
Marian, how could you do this to me, when I'm your dearest Uncle?

MARIAN
I wanted to show you, Uncle, that the Sheriff is not as clever as he thinks.

PRINCE
Curse you, Sheriff! You didn't catch Robin Hood, and you made me give up a whole year of taxes for nothing!

Prince John suddenly becomes energetic and chases the Sheriff offstage, yelling.

PRINCE
(as he chases the Sheriff)
You've lost me a lot of gold! Wait till I get my hands on you!

SHERIFF
(as he runs for his life)
But it was such a clever plan! And I wanted that gold, too!

> *Jujubee runs off. The Ladies,*
> *Guards and Captain follow.*

JUJUBEE
(as he follows the Prince)
I never knew the Prince could move so fast! Woo-hoo!

GUARDS, CAPTAIN
(ad lib as they follow Jujubee)
Watch out, Sheriff! Look at him run! Get him!

LADIES
(ad lib as they follow Jujubee)
Ooh, I love a good chase! Humph! He deserves to be yelled at!

> *The Merry Band is left onstage.*
> *Robin crosses to Marian and*
> *bows to her.*

ROBIN
Thank you, that was amazing.

MARIAN
Can you tell I've been practicing, like you said?

OUTLAWS
Yes!

ROBIN
(to Outlaws)
Let's welcome the newest member of the Merry Band, the Lady Marian—

SCARLETT
If she's going to be an outlaw, we can't be calling her "Lady" all the time.

ALAN-A
That's right, we can't. How about Miss Marian?

MUCH
Dame Marian?

HAWK
Madam Marian?

LITTLE JOHN
Hey-you Marian?

FRIAR TUCK
No, we're not all as rude as you are.

LITTLE JOHN
Who're you calling rude?

FRIAR TUCK
You, ya big clodhopper!

> *Little John and Friar Tuck face off one last time. Robin interrupts and they break apart.*

ROBIN
I know! What about Maid Marian?

MARIAN
Maid Marian! I like it!

ALAN-A
Ahem!
(sings on key for a change)
Ma-a-a-a-aid, Maid Marian!

> *The Outlaws and Marian applaud in astonishment.*

ROBIN
So let's hear it for Maid Marian!

OUTLAWS
Huzzah!

MARIAN
And let's hear it for Robin Hood—

ROBIN
—and all the Merry Band!

ALL
Huzzah!

Music 09: Finale: Our Merry Band
Vocal chorus, instrumental interlude, vocal half-chorus

OUTLAWS, ROBIN, MARIAN
Come, lasses and lads,
Take leave of your dads
And off to the forest flee.
In Sherwood fair you'll find us there
For an outlaw band are we.

MARIAN
We take from the rich and sleek
And give to the poor and meek.

ROBIN
When Marian lets her arrows fly,
The villains will run and cry.

OUTLAWS, ROBIN, MARIAN
Our Merry Band is taking a stand,
For justice throughout the land.

Interlude: The Merry Band
carouses to the music. Alan-a
"plays" a recorder.

OUTLAWS, ROBIN, MARIAN
We take from the rich and sleek
And give to the poor and meek.
When Robin lets his/her arrows fly,
The villains all run and cry.
Our Merry Band is taking a stand,
For justice throughout the land.

The Merry Band (including
Marian) ends the song in a
heroic but jolly pose.

THE END

ABOUT THE AUTHORS

Valerie Speaks and Dale Jones are a married couple, and have performed (separately and together) for many years in dinner and community theaters throughout Southern California. Valerie is a professional writer of corporate training materials, while Dale works as a director and teacher in children's theater.

Their scripts have been produced at venues such as:
- GO-FAME Youth Theatre Company (Long Beach, California)
- All the Arts for All the Kids Summer and After-School Programs (Fullerton, California)
- All-American Melodrama Theatre (formerly in Long Beach, California)

Made in the USA
Columbia, SC
04 November 2021